Retiring?
Beware!!

Don't Run out of Money and
Don't Become Bored

Retiring?
Beware!!

Don't Run out of Money and Don't Become Bored

Michael Bivona, CPA

RETIRING? BEWARE!!
DON'T RUN OUT OF MONEY AND DON'T BECOME BORED

iUniverse books may be ordered through booksellers or by contacting:

iUniverse
1663 Liberty Drive
Bloomington, IN 47403
www.iuniverse.com
1-800-Authors (1-800-288-4677)

Because of the dynamic nature of the Internet, any web addresses or links contained in this book may have changed since publication and may no longer be valid. The views expressed in this work are solely those of the author and do not necessarily reflect the views of the publisher, and the publisher hereby disclaims any responsibility for them.

Any people depicted in stock imagery provided by Thinkstock are models, and such images are being used for illustrative purposes only.
Certain stock imagery © Thinkstock.

ISBN: 978-1-4917-5202-9 (sc)
ISBN: 978-1-4917-5201-2 (e)

Library of Congress Control Number: 2014921697

Print information available on the last page.

iUniverse rev. date: 06/18/2015

CONTENTS

PREFACE

I retired at age 63 in 1997. Like most people nearing retirement, my main concern was having enough money to continue a lifestyle similar to, or better than, the one we had when I was gainfully employed. Like most people, we wanted to enjoy traveling and hobbies without worrying about skimping or running out of funds, and if possible, to have ample resources to help support our favorite charities and hopefully enough left over after our time on earth, to leave some money to our children and grandchildren.

Since I can look back over the last 20 years, I have the advantage of discussing the successful and not so successful financial strategies that my friends and I have lived through. While most writers of retirement books take a philosophical approach to advising their audience about the best methods to a successful retirement, I will base my writings on personal experiences and the impact that financial communities such as banks, the stock markets, and governmental policies had on our retirement plans.

What we should keep in mind is that—according to a television interview that House Speaker John Boehner had on September 19, 2011 and subsequently repeated in an article in a March, 2014 newsletter by A. Barry Rand, CEO of AARP: "More than 10,000 baby boomers will be reaching retirement age every day, a trend that is expected to continue for the next 16 years." Barry Rand also added that "people turning 50 today may have more than half of their life ahead of them."

Considering that between 3 and 4 million people a year will be retiring now and in the near future, it becomes increasingly important that pre-retirees and retirees get their retirement planning under control to enable them to have an active and financially secure retirement. Based on my years as a New York Certified

Public Accountant, financial advisor, Chief Financial Officer of a major computer enhancement company and my almost 20 years in retirement, I hope that my experiences will be of help in guiding people in their retirement planning.

My writings are not meant to advise people in financial matters or how to keep busy during retirement; my objective is to show how my wife Barbara and I planned for our retirement and managed to succeed in most of our planning.

Throughout my book, I strongly suggest that qualified professional advisors become an integral part of developing the financial planning of retirees.

ACKNOWLEDGMENTS

How can I begin to thank my three-year-old grandson, Michael Bivona Gharib, for revitalizing my 80-year old body and mind? His good nature and ever-present smile and his love for Pa and Grandma begin and end our days with bright anticipation for our next Skype encounter or live meetings.

I must also thank my wife of over 50 years, Barbara, for her patience, good nature, and her ever-present smile, and fortunately, for her love for Pa. I must also thank her for Michael's obviously inherited pleasant disposition.

C H A P T E R   O N E

Developing Retirement Plans

There is no doubt that retiring with financial security in the 21st century is complicated and in many cases illusory. People look forward to retirement as that time of life where they are free to do all the fun things that were unobtainable or rare while employed and raising a family. It's visualized as "Our time of life," free from the responsibilities that were required when earning a living and guiding one's children to a place in life where they were safely on their own. When looking at our circumstances and those of our retired friends, we readily determined that devoting all of one's time to the betterment of one's self is not always a reality easily attained. Money, health, and personal obligations usually dictate how much time can be spent in fulfilling all or part of our retirement expectations.

One of the most important things to consider is that you have to have something to retire to. Before retiring, it's wise to begin building bridges to things you are passionate about so that when the time comes, you have a choice of which bridges you can comfortably take into the next chapter of your life.

When the first U.S. Census was conducted in 1790, only 2% of the population was over 65 years of age. In 1900, the average American age was only 47. People who made it to 100 were considered an anomaly. Today, people that live to 100 have become common, as there are more than 100,000 of them in the United States as of this writing and the number is accelerating. The 2010 Census showed that the number of people aged 90 and older nearly tripled over the past three decades, reaching 1.9 million. It is estimated that in the next four decades this population will quadruple. The majority of people 90 and older are reported to have one or more disabilities and are predominately women. According to the latest statistics, over 14 million men and 20 million-plus women are over the age of 65, many of whom may live 20, 30, or even 40 years after retiring, which makes it imperative that future plans and bucket lists should certainly be made well in advance of retirement.

Due to the extended life expectancy in the 21st century and beyond, the traditional definition of retirement itself has become convoluted. When I was a young man, retirement meant that I would spend my remaining days on earth in the pursuit of leisurely activities and that this would probably last for only a few years. But today, considering that many retirees might have as many years in the retirement phase of their lives as they did working, the big question is how to put that precious time to productive and gratifying use.

Baby Boomers, of which there are estimated to be over 70 million that are headed for the last stage of their lives, have abandoned the word retirement and have replaced it with *rewirement*. They have even abandoned "the last stage of their lives" for "the beginning of a new life," which they expect to last 20 or more years. So, how does one prepare to be rewired?

I discuss "Life Reimagined" in Chapter Nine. It's a good starting place to explore the possibilities of "the beginning of a new life" as the old one approaches its end.

CHAPTER TWO

Since the Beginning of the New Millennium—Year 2000— and its Impact on Retirees

Although it may seem like "old hat," I think it would be appropriate to rehash some events that have taken place since the beginning of the new millennium that were caused by the financial communities that brought the world's stock markets to its knees and forever changed the retirement plans of hundreds of millions of people around the world. I'm not attempting to give my readers a history lesson, but I feel it's imperative from the outset that my position on retirees "playing the stock market" should be expressed. Most people contemplating retirement have one thing in common: They want a safe steady flow of income during their retirement years. How they go about realizing their goals is a whole other story. It is my hope that my experiences and financial background will be helpful in guiding seniors in their choices for a more financially secure retirement.

On the first day of the Millennium, a headline in the *New York Times* stated, "Stocks End the Year on an Up Note." It went on to report:

> In a week with relatively little news other than
> fears of Y2K, (which was the day that all computers
> were to crash due to a digital flaw in the dates), the

Dow Jones industrial average broke two records last week—the second coming on the final day of trading. The Dow closed Friday at 11,497, giving it a 25 percent return for the year. The return is considered above average under most standards—and continues the streak of returns above 20 percent for the Dow—but it pales in comparison to the astounding finish for the NASDAQ composite index and its host of technology companies. The NASDAQ ended the year at a record 4,069.29, an astounding return of nearly 86 percent. The index's 1999 return is the largest ever for a U.S. stock index.

Life was good: crime had fallen, stocks had soared, and the Treasury was actually running a surplus. All we had to worry about was whether there were bugs in our computers that would bring the world's electronic babies crashing down at precisely midnight on December 31, 1999.

By January 14, 2000, the Dow peaked at 11,723. NASDAQ followed, when it hit its all-time high of 5,132.52. By the end of the year, the indices bottomed at 10,788 for the Dow and an astonishing drop for NASDAQ to 2,470.52. It was the beginning of every investor's nightmare. In 2001, the NASDAQ lost an additional 21.05%, going from 2,470.52 to 1,950.40. It continued to crumble in 2002, when it bottomed out at 1,108.49—a 78.4% drop from its all-time high of 5,132.52. The Dow Jones Industrial Average followed, ending at 10,021 in 2001 and an unpredicted drop to 8,341 in 2002, for a 28.85% drop from its peak of 11,723.

The decrease in stock value from the 2000 crash is estimated to have been in excess of 8 trillion dollars. Needless to say, the impact on people contemplating retirement was devastating. Many postponed their plans, while others had to come out of retirement and return to the workforce—if they could find employment. Some of the causes of the crash that **so-called experts** have determined were:

- **Corporate corruption.** Many companies fraudulently inflated their profits and used accounting loopholes to hide debt.

Corporate officers enjoyed outrageous stock options that diluted company stock.

- **Overvalued stocks.** Many companies that had large losses with no hope of turning a profit reported profits and market capitalization of billions of dollars.
- **Day traders and momentum investors.** The advent of the Internet enabled online trading as an inexpensive way to **play the stock market**. This revolution led to millions of new investors and traders entering the markets with little or no experience.
- **Conflict of Interest between Research Firm Analysts and Investment Bankers.** It was a common practice for the research departments of investment banks to give favorable ratings on securities for which their clients sought to raise money. Many companies received favorable ratings, even though they were actually having financial problems.

One would think, that after suffering over 8 trillion dollars of devalued assets in the stock market worldwide, that people would have learned some sort of lesson after the Crash of 2000 and would have shied away from investing in corporate America securities. Greed and unrealistic dreams, however, seem to overcome good sense when getting rich fast in the stock market is concerned. In the year 2008, we saw a repeat performance of the 2000-2002 crash that probably equaled if not exceeded the loss of wealth witnessed by the former Panic Crash. It wasn't surprising that the same excuses mentioned above were again given for the additional trillions of dollars that were lost.

Today, in 2014, the stock exchanges are again reaching all-time highs because people are pouring money—including retirement funds—into stocks and bonds that promise higher returns than the paltry 1%, or less, that banks are paying. It should be interesting to see where the financial exchanges are by the time this book is published, and the effect that they will have on retirees and the 70+ million baby boomers that are contemplating retiring.

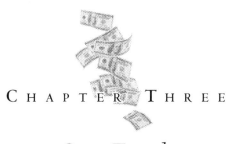

C H A P T E R   T H R E E

Our Family

A little history of my family will show that we have a lot in common with most readers. My beautiful wife Barbara is 76 years young. She was born in Brownsville, Brooklyn, New York and lived in that neighborhood for the first 20 years of her life. When we met, she was living in the renowned former Brooklyn Dodgers' section of Brooklyn on Flatbush Avenue, on the first floor of a relatively new high-rise building. It is said that the three most important things in finding the right place to live are "**location, location, location.**" Well, she certainly found the **right** place to live; it was two blocks from Brooklyn's pride and joy, Prospect Park, where we spent many leisurely summer afternoons rowing on its gigantic lake, walking through beautiful Technicolor gardens, and picnicking around—lunch basket, blanket, and wine in hand—on the spacious grass areas. Just one block from her apartment was the Rutland Road subway train station where she caught the train to Manhattan each morning to begin her workday. She was employed as a secretary and financial manager at Rugoff Theaters and subsequently at an advertising firm that specialized in theater advertising. The only downside to the "L-shaped" apartment was the subway train approaching the Rutland Road Station that ran alongside the rooms and mercilessly vibrated the whole unit, which consisted of a small kitchen, a very small dining room, a nice-sized living room, a small alcove bedroom, and a very modern but small bathroom. Barbara attended Brooklyn College, majoring in astronomy with a minor in geology. While in attendance, she wrote for various news publications. My beautiful wife-to-be was also an accomplished pianist and a passionate guitarist when we met.

We were introduced to each other at the offices of Rugoff Theaters, which were located at 1270 Avenue of the Americas, in Manhattan. She was employed as a financial manager at Rugoff Theaters' home office. The building was adjacent to Radio City Music Hall and a part of the Rockefeller Plaza Center Complex. Her boss, Mr. Rugoff, was one of the first to present art movies in New York City, and showed great first-run exclusive movies such as *GIGI*, James Bond movies, and many Japanese art films, some of which played in two theaters simultaneously, which was an experiment in theater presentation in the 1950s. His 15 movie houses, which included some of the first multiplex theaters in the metropolitan area, kept Barbara busy keeping track of their financial records.

My job as an auditor with a certified public accounting firm was to review Barbara's work, and review I did. It became my favorite place to work, as I was captivated by her winning smile and charming character. We spent many lunch hours watching people ice skating in the winter at the Rockefeller Ice Skating Rink, which was around the corner from her office, shopping at Saks Fifth Avenue Department Store, which was a couple of blocks away, and at the underground mall that ran beneath Rockefeller Plaza. On payday, which was Friday of every week, when we had some extra *shekels,* we would hang around the bar at the Rainbow Room in the NBC building across from Radio City Music Hall, and literally rub shoulders with fellow New Yorkers, who were packed around the smoke-filled bar four deep and enjoying every moment of the discomfort. At that magical time of our lives, we also spent many enjoyable evenings dining on Restaurant Row, which is on 46th Street, between 7th and 8th Avenues, devouring the *cuisine* at the French, Italian, Spanish, and Russian restaurants, and attending many Broadway shows for free thanks to Barbara's connections in the entertainment industry. What a magical time to be in our mid-twenties, working in the heart of Manhattan and in love with the time, place, and energy of the most exciting city in the world, and **passionately in love with each other.**

At this writing, I'm 80-years of age. I was born in the East New York section of Brooklyn and spent my formative years at several different residences throughout the borough. At the age of 18, I enlisted in the United States Air Force in anticipation of my presence shortening the Korean War. My most memorable days were the two years spent in Japan as a Communication Specialist. I was fortunate to spend my last year in Tokyo as a liaison at the Imperial Palace, overseeing the Japanese personnel who were using communication equipment that was the property of the United States. After completing my four years in the service of the United States, I attended Long Island University, located in downtown Brooklyn, New York, majoring in accounting with a minor in economics. After completing my tour of duty at the university, I worked for a certified public accounting firm in Manhattan, New York, and was fortunate to be assigned to their Rugoff Theater account. That is where I met my soul mate and life partner, Barbara Selden. A couple of years later, we were married and moved from Barbara's apartment in Brooklyn to Menlo Park in New Jersey, where, with the help of Barbara's good cooking and her scholastic drilling skills, I passed the New York State Certified Public Accounting examinations. In short order, we were back in the Empire State setting up house in Dix Hill on Long Island, where we still reside with no plans of moving.

After a few years of marriage, we were blessed with our son Stephen Paul, and a little over a year later we were also blessed with our daughter, Laurie Jo, who completed our family unit. In time, I started my own accounting firm and eventually had offices in Melville and then Massapequa, Long Island, practicing under the name of Bivona, Ambrico, and Dlugacz, Certified Public Accountants. After 25-years in the accounting business, I retired from the profession and became a part owner of Manchester Technologies, which was located in Hauppauge, Long Island. The 12 years I spent with the computer enhancement company went by quickly, and at age 63, when our organization became a public company trading on NASDAQ, I was able to retire on a fulltime basis.

Developing a Social Network While Making Your Bucket List a Reality

Before discussing my thoughts about the financial aspects of retiring, I thought that I should write about how we built bridges before retiring so we could experience some of our passions that were listed on our Bucket List, and how we've been able to achieve many of our goals over the last 20-years, without becoming bored.

Senior Civic Centers

Civic centers can be found in almost every municipality in the United States. Most of these centers usually have a department dedicated to the betterment of the senior citizens that live within their confines. Barbara and I are fortunate to have wonderfully progressive centers in nearby towns where we live in New York and Florida.

In Florida, we have the use of the Boynton Beach Senior Center, which is indicative of most modern senior centers in the United States. How progressive they are is easily determined by visiting their website. Here is a small example of their forward thinking, which I gleaned from their Civic Center Information Bulletin:

Just for Boomers and Seniors!

Developing Programs for the Baby Boomer Generation

With strong spirits and aging bodies, Baby Boomers are changing the face of recreation. They have rewritten the rules through every life stage and they will do it again. The Boynton Beach Recreation and Parks Department is ready to take on the boomers at the Senior Center and in all the recreation programs. With input from newly or son-to-be retirees, we will break through traditional norms to meet the demands of this generation in order to develop adult-focused activities that encompass the social and physical interest of this dynamic age group. Contact us today with any program ideas that you'd like to share that will engage Boynton Boomers!

The bulletin continues:

Just For Seniors

Did you know that the Boynton Beach Senior Center offers free membership to all Boynton Beach residents within its city limits ages 55+? There are numerous activities and events throughout the year that attract hundreds of monthly and thousands of yearly participants. For many of the participating patrons, the Senior Center is a place to socialize and feel needed, a place to stimulate minds, play pool, have a meal, or learn about computers. It has changed lives and improved the quality of life for many seniors living in Boynton Beach and the surrounding areas.

As can be determined from the above information, there is no doubt that a good starting place for people that want to socialize and meet others in their age group would be senior centers. In our experience, we have had the opportunity to participate in group dance classes, have watched bridge card tournaments, played checkers and chess, as well as attended craft classes and most excitingly, have been members of adventurous tours, specially geared for seniors, with all the necessary comforts such as plush seating on buses, knowledgeable docents, and frequent rest stops.

A great website to further explore prospects available for seniors is "Fun Activities for Senior Citizens." Some of the opportunities discussed are:

> **Silver Sneakers**—is a program that offers Medicare-eligible adults membership in participating fitness centers. This program encourages healthy living through fitness classes, social gathering, and seminars on healthy living. Seniors can also have access to a program advisor and online support to help address seniors' unique health needs.
>
> **Hobbies**—what better time to consider taking up a hobby that you never had time to enjoy? Why not try:

- Arts and crafts
- Jewelry making
- Scrapbooking
- Photography
- Gourmet cooking
- Sewing/quilting
- Raised bed gardening

A pleasant experience that we had at the Florida center was when my wife Barbara joined a group of ladies in costume jewelry making. The artists—and to see some of their creations justifies the title—meet a couple of times a month to create and exchange ideas in how to improve their masterpieces. The six girls rotate locations, from home to home, and spend afternoons beading while enjoying a variety of coffees and sweets. Interestingly, the artists are also our dancing friends—which goes to prove that a first step in the right directions can lead to many new roads to travel in life. Three of the ladies are French Canadians that spend their winters in Florida. That fact has added another dimension to opening doors as visiting each other has become a vacation we look forward to during the summer months. An interesting aside is that the American English speaking girls are learning some French expressions and the French Canadian girls are fine-tuning their English skills. Another snowball effect that has developed is that a couple of times a month we rotate dinner parties—and let me tell you, I'm of Italian decent and love my wife's Italian-Russian cuisine, but having French homemade cooking has become one of my favorite culinary delights.

To continue with the website's suggestions, other things seniors should try are:

> **Music**—music nourishes the brain. A study by Brenda Hanna-Pladdy, PhD, and Alicia Mackay, PhD, found that seniors who played musical instruments performed better on cognitive tests than those who did not play an instrument.
>
> If you have always wanted to learn to play a trumpet, saxophone, or guitar, go to your local music store and ask about private lessons for senior beginners. Better yet, check out New Horizons International Music Association (NHIMA), a non-profit organization that provides entry points to music making for adults, including those with no musical experience as well as those who were once musically active but have not been so for a long time.

In Chapter four, my wife Barbara's story, *Chicken Soup and Chocolate Pudding,* tells of a retired senior who realized his dream by taking trumpet lessons, that led to playing in a band and finally, having his own award winning band in New York. This was accomplished when he began his new career after retiring.

The list on "Fun Activities for Senior Citizens" is endless. So I'll end with their final suggestion:

Finally, Celebrate Life!

Now is the time to do the things you love. Figure out which activities make you the happiest, make a list, and dive in. Don't be afraid to explore new activities, especially if it's something you have always wanted to do. Enjoy your time as an independent senior and *let the good times roll!*

Dancing

Barbara and I have always been fascinated by people who could get on a dance floor and dance to whatever music was being played, whether it was Latin, Smooth, or just Social Dancing. They seemed to dance with confidence and style and had an air about them that said, "There isn't anything else that I would rather be doing." We always seemed to enjoy whatever little dancing we did at weddings and social events, but never got the hang of doing routines that made sense or would make us feel that we had accomplished anything resembling what other good dancers could do. So when we got close to retirement, we decided to give dancing a chance and started looking for a reputable dance instructor who would help us begin our new journey.

Finding a qualified, honest dance studio or instructor was a challenge. Many dance studios, but not all, try to sign new students to long-term contracts costing thousands of dollars, and when the training begins, the instructors teach more than one dance at the same time, which in many cases confuses the students. One of the major problems with long-term contracts, which can run up to one or more years, is that if the students aren't happy with their progress or instructors, they are obliged to continue under the terms of their contract, resulting in many students quitting and losing their money. So it's important that if dancing is in the future for retirees, they should sign with a reputable dance studio or instructor and arrange to learn one dance at a time on a **pay-as-you-go basis**. To save money and experiment to see if dancing is something that a person is interested in, check out some of the many dance halls that give free group lessons before general dancing begins. The prices of entry to these facilities are usually in the 10 to 15 dollar range and often include refreshments, dessert, and in some instances a light meal.

We decided to take our first lessons at Swing Street Studio, which was owned and operated by the talented Elektra Underhill. Our arrangement was that we would take a couple of Swing dance lessons and if we were pleased, we would continue until we were happy with our progress. Well, that was the beginning of a life-long relationship with Elektra and the local dance community, of which she seemed to be the *prima donna.* In time, we would become an integral part of that community and our lifestyles would be more or less directed by the activities and events within the social network. It took some time for me to get over my macho persona and accept the constructive criticism that was a part of the learning experience. But in time, with Elektra and Barbara's patience, I learned to behave myself and progress and I loved every step of the journey.

Our dance group had review sessions twice a week at her studio, which allowed us to practice the routines we learned and to switch partners to get the feeling of how others interpreted what each had learned. We also planned our social dancing excursions at various dance halls together and traveled to dance exhibitions and shows as a family. The uniqueness of belonging to a group where everyone has the same common passion of being happy while expressing themselves in dance is a life-changing experience and should certainly be tried by everyone with a desire to fill in the spare time that retirees find they have in abundance when they begin their journey into their **Golden Years.**

To give retirees an idea of what a dancing community is like and the opportunities that dancers have to join in popular dance events and to meet some of the world's famous dancers, I decided to extract from the back of my mind one of the most memorable nights that Barbara and I had at a show in the local Suburban Center in Wantagh,

Long Island, NY., which was sponsored by Louis Del Prete, dance instructor and promoter extraordinaire.

Barbara and I were fortunate to have seen two shows sponsored by Louis featuring couples from *Dancing with the Stars*. We saw Karina Smirnoff and Louie Van Amstel on May 31, 2008, and the husband and wife team of Edyta Sliwinska and Alec Mazo on May 30, 2009. Needless to say, both shows were spectacular and played to full houses of over 400 dance lovers. Although the venue was small, the enthusiasm in which the audience received both events was quite large.

The exhibition that stands out in my mind is Karina and Louie's epic and passionate display of **dancing personified.** Karina and Louie go back to the year 2000, when they won the U.S. National Latin Championship, the Can-Am DanceSport Gala-Canadian open Professional Championship in International Latin, the Japan International Dancing Championship for Professional Latin, and the prestigious Emerald Ball DanceSport Championship for Open Professional Latin. That was certainly a busy and rewarding year for the new dancing partnership.

They were introduced by Louis and received a roaring welcome from the eager audience. Their first dance was Jive. The speed of the dance and the aerobic moves that they performed seemed unreal as they moved in a circle in the middle of the dance floor. Karina's short white dress and flowing legs against Louie's black suit were a contrast in perfection as they jived in unison to the beats of the fast music. Their next dance was a romantic Rumba. They performed a "chicky-chicky-boom" to the rhythm of the music with sexy sways and *cortes*; the room heated from their sensual rubs and caresses. You could almost see the steam coming from her long white open-backed dress, which was complemented by his tight black pants and black, wide-open shirt. When watching romantic performances and getting caught up in the heat of the moment, it's easy to understand why many people prefer to call ballroom dancing an "Art Form" rather than an athletic endeavor. My opinion is that it's both: an athletic event when required, and an "Art Form" when desired.

To continue the romantic mood, they performed a spicy Tango. The heat again radiated from their movements and filled the hall; it seemed that energy burst from her body and through her long black semi-opened shoulder dress, sparked by his shirtless tuxedo showing his chest, bordered by the jacket's velvet lapels. The smooth sways and caresses followed by quick turns and kicks clearly transmitted the essence of the dance: flirtation, chase, seduction, and then finally, conquest. It all happened before our eyes; it appeared to be a dress rehearsal of a passionate affair, which the audience approved of and confirmed with their spontaneous oohs and aahs, and then a standing ovation.

Their final dance was a Cha-Cha. They exploded onto the dance floor and went full speed ahead into the dance with arms flying and legs moving almost as fast as the speed of light. Their quick movements and acrobatic gyrations didn't resemble a conventional Cha-Cha, but then these were not conventional dancers—they were world champions and performed the dance as champions should, with moves that were far beyond ordinary. Their speed caused her yellow short sleeveless and backless dress bottom to swirl when she spun around, resembling a Hawaiian hula skirt. His open black shirt, displaying his manly chest, added to the energy of the dance.

It's commonly known that "a picture is worth a thousand words," so below are two pictures, the first of Karina and Louie, followed by Edyta and Alec, of their performances at the Suburban Center. While looking at the photos, one can almost feel the energy of their movements radiating from the pictures. The photos are presented below, with Louis Del Prete's permission:

After the audience calmed down from Karina and Louie's exhibition and the couple had a chance to rest, they returned for a "Question and Answer" session. The first question from the audience was directed at Karina:

> Which of the Mario's do you like best? Twenty-three-year-old R&B star Mario Barrett, from the sixth season of DWTS, or the 33-year-old television heartthrob Mario Lopez, from the third season of DWTS?

After blushing and snickering, Karina answered:

> I've been seeing Mario Lopez for some time, and there is nothing and has never been anything but a professional relationship between me and the younger Mario.

Question for Louie:

> How long does it take to create the beautiful girl's outfits and the men's clothing?

Louie answered:

> The designers are given their tasks on Tuesday and they must have the outfits fitted and completed by Friday of the same week, which is a major undertaking by a staff of exceptional designers and craftspeople.

Question for Karina:

> Who chooses which dances are to be performed by the couples?

Karina answered:

ABC has a special staff of knowledgeable dance professionals that choose which couples are to perform each of the dances.

Question for Louie:

Who chooses the music for the dances that are performed on DWTS?

Louie answered:

ABC has a special staff that chooses the music for the dances and are guided by some of the professional dancers in the choice of music that each couple will perform to. In many cases, the music is not what is usually heard when dancing to specific dances, which makes performing the dances a lot more difficult.

Question for Louie:

Is it true that the performing celebrities receive $200,000 per season and an additional bonus if they win the Mirror Ball Trophy?

Louie answered:

That sounds about right.

Question for Karina:

Who chooses the celebrities' professional partners?

Karina answered:

ABC chooses the partners based on a random selection, with no preference to a guest's talent.

Question for Louie:

Do you create your own choreography?

Louie answered:

Yes, I also do many of the group's choreography for the show and I'm also the Creative Director. It's very challenging to get twenty or so professionals to dance as a group, but the outcome is always a rewarding experience. When performing, I'm also responsible for the dance routines for me and my partner. Each of the professionals is required to do the arranging for their own dance routines once they are given the music and their dance assignments from ABC. So the professionals, in addition to being champion dancers, must also be proficient choreographers.

Question for Karina:

How long are the contracts between ABC and the professional dancers?

Karina answered:

Our contracts run through 2015, but that doesn't mean that all the professionals will appear on all the shows; we are actually on standby.

Another question for Karina:

How much notice do the professionals get before they have to appear on the show?

Karina answered:

One month.

Another question for Karina:

How much notice do the celebrities get from ABC to prepare for the show?

Karina answered:

Two to three months.

After the question and answers session, Karina and Louie were gracious enough to remain at the center for a couple of hours to pose for pictures with their admirers. The line was too long, so Barbara and I decided that we would postpone the picture taking for another time. Much to the delight of the dance community, the couple remained on Long Island for a few days and conducted private and group dance lessons for the benefit of their fans. We would catch up with Karina during her exhibition at Gold Coast Ballroom in Coconut Creek, Florida later on that year. I not only got to dance with the charming beauty, but we had our picture taken with her when we presented her with a signed copy of my book, *Dancing Around the World with Mike and Barbara Bivona,* in which photos, including the above, are featured. A picture of her receiving my book follows:

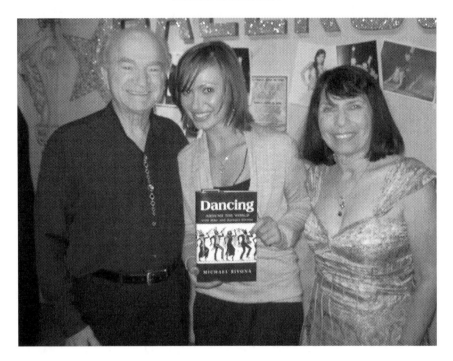

The snowball effect of our taking dancing lessons before retiring went from the first lesson, to meeting many new dancing friends, to many dance cruises around the world, to writing a book about dancing, and finally, to meeting and dancing with the *crème-de-la-crème* of the dance world. The peripheral effects were my wife's beading sessions with our dancing friends, learning a little French from our Canadian neighbors, and my all-time favorite, the dinner engagements we shared, especially looking forward to the French *cuisine.*

The intellectual and mental benefits of dancing are rarely considered by the general population. There is no doubt that dancing is considered a physical activity, so much so that it's expected to become an Olympic event in the near future. But little has been written about the effect that dancing has on one's mental condition. I came across an article by Richard Powers, world-renowned scholar and an expert on American Social Dancing that will hopefully set the stage for more people becoming aware of the intellectual advantages of dancing. With Richard Powers' permission, I'm presenting his thoughts; it's our hope that with mental enhancements thrown into the formula, more people will take up the challenge and enter the world of ballroom dancing:

Use it or Lose It: Dancing Makes you Smarter, by Richard Powers

For hundreds of years dance manuals and other writings have lauded the health benefits of dancing, usually as physical exercise. We have also seen research on further health benefits of dancing, such as stress reduction and increased serotonin levels, with its sense of well-being. Recently we've heard of another benefit; it seems that frequent dancing apparently makes us smarter. A major study has added to the growing evidence that stimulating one's mind can ward off Alzheimer's disease and other dementia.

You've probably heard about the *New England Journal of Medicine* report on the effects of recreational activities on the mental acuity in aging. If you're not familiar with the study, here it is in a nutshell:

'The 21-year study of senior citizens, 75 and older, was led by the Albert Einstein College of Medicine in New York City, funded by the national Institute of Aging, and published in the *New England Journal of Medicine*. Their method for objectively measuring mental acuity in aging was to monitor rates of dementia, including Alzheimer's disease.

The study wanted to see if any physical or cognitive recreational activities influenced mental acuity. They discovered that some activities had a significant beneficial effect; others had none.

They studied cognitive activities such as reading books, writing for pleasure, doing crossword puzzles, playing cards, and playing musical instruments. They also studied physical activities like playing tennis, golf, swimming, bicycling, dancing, walking for exercise, and doing housework.

One of the surprises of the study was that almost none of the physical activities appeared to offer any protection against dementia. There can be cardiovascular benefits of course, but the focus of this study was the mind. There was one important exception: the only physical activity to offer protection against dementia was frequent dancing. The results were:

Bicycling and swimming – 0%
Dancing frequently – 76% reduced risk of dementia
Playing golf – 0%
Reading – 35% reduced risk of dementia

Dancing without a doubt has the greatest risk reduction of any activity studied, cognitive or physical.

Aging and Memory:

When brain cells die and synapses weaken with aging, our nouns go first, like names of people, because there's only one neural pathway connecting to that stored information. If the single neural connection to that name fades, we lose access to it. So, as we age, we learn to parallel process, to come up with synonyms to go around these roadblocks. (Or maybe we don't learn to do this, and just become a dimmer light bulb.) The key here is that more is better. Do whatever you can to create new neural paths. The opposite of this is taking the same old well-worn path over and over again, with habitual patterns of thinking.

When I was studying the creative process as a grad student at Stanford, I came across a perfect analogy to this: 'The more stepping stones there are across a creek, the easier it is to cross in your own style.'

The focus of that aphorism was creative thinking, to find as many alternative paths as possible to a creative solution, but as we age, parallel processing becomes more critical. Now it's no longer a matter of style, it's a matter of survival—getting across the creek at all. Randomly dying brain cells are like stepping stones being removed one by one. Those who had only one well-worn path of stones are completely blocked when some are removed. But those who spent their lives trying different mental routes, creating a myriad of possible paths, still had several paths left. The Albert Einstein College of Medicine study shows that we need to keep as many of those paths active as we can, while also generating new paths, to maintain the complexity of our neuronal synapses.

Considering the research, we immediately ask two questions: Why is dancing better than other activities for improving mental capabilities? And does this mean all kinds of dancing, or is one kind of dancing better than another?

The essence of intelligence is making decisions. And the concluding advice, when it comes to improving your mental acuity, is to involve yourself in activities which require split-second rapid-fire decisions, as opposed to rote memory (retracing the same well-worn path), or just working on your physical style.

One way to accomplish this is to learn something new. Not just dancing, but anything new. Don't worry about the probability that you'll never use it in the future. Take a class to challenge your mind. It will stimulate the connectivity of your brain by generating the need for new pathways. Difficult and even frustrating classes are better for you, as they will create a greater need for new neural pathways.

Take a dance class, which can really stimulate your mind. Dancing integrates several brain functions at once, thereby increasing connectivity. Dancing simultaneously involves kinesthetic, rational, musical, and emotional processes.

The question then is: what kind of dancing?

Let's go back to the study: bicycling, swimming, or playing golf – 0% reduced risk of dementia.

But doesn't golf require rapid-fire decision-making? No, not if you're a long-time player. You made most of the decisions when you first started playing, years ago. Now the game is mostly refining your technique. It can be good physical exercise, but the study showed it led to no improvement in mental acuity.

So taking the kinds of dance classes where you must make as many spit-second decisions as possible is the key to maintaining true intelligence and reducing dementia.

Does any kind of dancing lead to increased mental acuity? No, not all forms of dancing will produce this benefit. Not dancing, which, like golf or swimming, mostly works on style or retracing the same memorized paths? The key is the decision-making and keeping in mind that intelligence is what we use when we don't already know what to do.

We wish that 25 years ago the Albert Einstein College of Medicine thought of doing side-by-side comparisons of different kinds of dancing to find out which was better. But we can figure it out by looking at who they studied: seniors 75 and older, beginning in 1980. Those who danced in that particular population were former Roaring Twenties dancers and former Swing Era dancers, so the kind of dancing most of them continued to do in retirement was what they began when they were young: freestyle social dancing—basic Foxtrot, Swing, Waltz, and Latin.

I've been watching senior citizens dancing all of my life, from my parents (who met at a Tommy

Dorsey dance), to retirement communities, to the Roseland Ballroom in New York City. I almost never see memorized sequence of patterns on the dance floor. I mostly see easygoing, fairly simple social dancing —freestyle leads and follows. But freestyle social dancing isn't that simple. It requires a lot of split-second decision-making, in both the lead and follow roles.

When it comes to preserving mental acuity, some forms of dancing are apparently better than others. When we talk of intelligence (use it or lose it), the more decision-making we bring into our dancing, the better.

Who benefits more, women or men?

In social dancing, the follow role automatically gains a benefit by having to make hundreds of split-second decisions as to what to do next. Women don't follow, they interpret the signals their partners are giving them, which requires intelligence and decision-making, which is active, and not passive. This benefit is greatly enhanced by dancing with different partners, not always the same leader. With different dance partners, you have to adjust much more and be aware of more variables. This is great for staying smarter longer.

But men, you can also match her degree of decision-making if you choose to do so by:

(1) Really notice your partner and what works best for her. Notice what is comfortable for her, where she is already going, which moves are successful with her and which aren't, and constantly adapt your dancing to these observations. That's rapid-fire split-second decision-making.

(2) Don't lead the same old patterns the same way each time. Challenge yourself to try new things. Make more decisions more often. And gentlemen, the huge side-benefit is that your partners will have much more

fun dancing with you when you are attentive to their dancing and constantly adjust for their comfort and continuity of motion.

Dance often:

Finally, remember that this study made another suggestion: Seniors who did crossword puzzles four days a week had a significantly lower risk of dementia than did those who did a puzzle once a week. So, if you can't take dance classes or go out dancing four times a week, then dance as much as you can; the more often the better.

I thought it would be appropriate to list some dancing sites that may be of interest to anyone considering experimenting with the fun world of dancing and the social networking opportunities that it offers:

USA Dance at www.usadance.org, formerly the United States Amateur Ballroom Association (USABDA):

There is an annual fee of $25 for social membership in one of its local chapters. The organization is worldwide and allows members to participate in dancing events locally and around the world. Its primary goals are:

To promote amateur DanceSport as a sport both nationally and internationally and to foster its inclusion in the Olympic and Pan American games; to organize and support amateur DanceSport events globally, including national, regional and local championships; and to select the top DanceSport athletes to represent the United States in the World DanceSport Amateur Championships and the world games and to finance their participation.

It's the foremost amateur dance organization in the United States and strives to "promote social dancing as a healthful lifetime recreational activity, suitable for individuals, families, and for those who are so inclined, it's a stepping stone into competition dancing." Some of its famous former amateur members can be found performing on ABC's *Dancing With the Stars*. The following are some of the professional dancers who were once amateur members of USA Dance and now appear on that popular television show:

Julianne Hough, **www.juliannehough.net**
Edyta Sliwinska, www.edytasliwinska.com
Anna Trebunskaya, **www.annatrebuskays.com**
Cheryl Burke, **www.cherylburkedance.com**
Lacey Schwimmer, **www.schwimmersthedancecenter.com**
Corky Ballas, **www.corky.com**
Mark Ballas, **www.markballas.com**
Derek Hough, **www.derekhough.net**
Alec Mazo, **www.alecmazo.com**
Brian Fortuna, **www.brianfortuna.com**

Other useful dance sites are:

World Pro-Am DanceSport Series, www. dancesportseries.com. This program features dance students; they hold over 70 competitions annually across the United States and encourage students on every level to participate.
AccessDance, www.accessdance.com. They provide a network site that finds dance lessons and venues for students and offers information on dance organizations, competitions, merchants, and publications.
DanceBeat International, www.dancebeat.com. They provide periodical highlights from competitive ballroom dancing around the world.

International Dance Directory, www.dancedirectory.com. They provide a worldwide directory of dancers, with sections for locating teachers, studios, and merchandise.

Ballroom Dancers, www.ballroomdancers.com. They are a clearinghouse for ballroom dancing information, including worldwide dancing locations and are a dance learning center for most recognized dances.

In my neck of the woods, New York City and Long Island, there are a couple of exceptional websites and studios for dancers of all levels; they are:

Touch Dancing Studios, www.touchdancing.com. Alfonso Triggiani is the director and owner of the Long Island studios. He is a renowned international dance aficionado and has his own television show, *Life Styles*, which features free dance lessons on Saturday mornings on New York City and Long Island channels.

Louis Del Prete, www.louisdelprete.com. He is a dance exhibition promoter, DJ extraordinaire, and top-of-the-line dance instructor. He sponsors and DJs themed dances throughout Long Island that always include free dance lessons prior to general dancing. He has promoted dance exhibitions with world-famous dancers in New York and Florida and is responsible for bringing some *Dancing With the Stars* professionals to local dance halls in both states. Some of his dance exhibitions have included: Karina Smirnoff and Louie Van Amstel, Edyta Sliwinska and her husband Alec Mazo, and Karina and Dmitry Chaplin. Louis is currently our New York teacher.

I think that retirees should give dancing a try, preferably before retirement. A few dance lessons will determine if it's a pastime that should be continued on a more social or serious level when time and family pressures are hopefully a thing of the past. Remember, each dance lesson builds blocks and adds to your brain's reserves, so that when blocks begin to disappear due to our natural aging process, there are hopefully ample reserves to replace the missing ones.

Sports – Tennis

I first became interested in tennis when I was in the United States Air Force. I was stationed at Nagoya Air Base in Japan, awaiting my next assignment, which would be for two years. While hanging around the base with not much to do, I met a young WAF (Women in the Air Force), Joan, who was wearing the cutest tennis outfit which complemented her picture-perfect gorgeous figure. We became friendly in a very short time; one of the benefits of our friendship was that she volunteered to teach me how to play tennis, which I thought at that time was a rich man's sport, based on the movies that I had seen where the rich and famous monopolized the game. So I made a beeline to the PX (Post Exchange) and bought all the necessary garments and equipment that would make me look like a bona fide tennis player. The look was okay, but the learning process was difficult and frustrating for a young twenty-year-old who thought that there was nothing in the world that he couldn't master. We played, at one thing or another, for the whole month that I was stationed at that base. Her advice to me, among many other words of wisdom, was, "Make sure you get a professional to teach you the game before you hurt yourself or some innocent bystander." I played on and off for two years while stationed in Tokyo. It was a great place to learn and enjoy the game, as almost every Japanese person I met was a devout tennis player and was willing to teach the young redhead the finer points of the game. There were many places to play; luckily for me, most venues were free to servicemen, which made the game all the more attractive, as a corporal's pay didn't go very far in those days. Unfortunately, I didn't take Joan's advice about hiring an instructor, as my pay scale didn't provide for that luxury, so although I looked good on the courts, my game was far from perfect. This gave many of the Japanese girls that I played with great satisfaction, as beating an American at anything was thought to be very honorable. For the short time that I played tennis, I made many new friends, which made my two year tour of duty in Tokyo go by not only quickly, but pleasantly, as many of my new Japanese friends invited me into their homes as an honorable guest.

After leaving the military when my four-year enlistment ended, I didn't have much opportunity to play again, as it was too expensive for a hard-working young underpaid person, and tennis courts were not readily available in my Brooklyn, NY neighborhood. It wasn't until attending Long Island University, in Brooklyn, that the opportunity to play again became available. There were tennis courts on the campus and I was finally able to follow Joan's advice, as instructors were available at very nominal fees, especially for ex-servicemen. So during my years at the university, whenever time allowed, I took lessons and played as much of the sport as I could fit into my tight schedule. After college, I played tennis very infrequently, as time, money, and opportunity rarely seemed to coincide with each other. When I had the time, then money or opportunity was scarce. When I had the money, then time or opportunity seemed to dictate that other priorities were more important. When I had the opportunity, then time or money seemed to be lacking. So time went by with me playing very little tennis until I married and had two children, Stephen and Laurie. When they were about ten and eleven years of age, they insisted that we take tennis lessons together. My wife Barbara also thought that a family sport would be a worthwhile way to spend quality time with our children. So we went to the indoor tennis courts that were in our neighborhood and began a series of tennis lessons that lasted three months. The kids loved the game, but Barbara and I just couldn't develop a passion for the sport; maybe our aged bodies were too set in their ways to introduce a new muscle stretcher into their routines. So the kids continued with their game while Barbara decided that shopping would be a better alternative.

It was surprising how many friends our children made while playing the game. It seemed that when they were not socializing with their tennis buddies, all of their spare time was spent on the tennis courts perfecting their game; a whole new social world opened to them due to the introduction of tennis into their lives.

Many of our friends are still playing tennis in their retirement years and couldn't imagine their lives without frequently sweating on the tennis courts. For my active friends, the passion of the game began with playing with newly found friends and on teams, and then graduated to attending games locally and then the ultimate tennis experience of traveling around the world to watch many of the Grand Slam tournaments that are hosted in Australia, France, England, and the United States.

There is an abundance of tennis locations that can be easily accessed on the website www.tennismaps.com. The site not only gives the location of courts, but actually allows for zooming onto an actual court of interest and outlines the details and rules for playing at a particular venue.

The cost of playing can be from zero, except for the cost of tennis balls, to expensive membership in fancy clubs, such as the Polo Club in Boca Raton, Florida. Many municipal and town parks have courts that residents can use at nominal or no charge that also may accommodate nonresidents. Another aspect of the sport is the wheelchair games. The sport began in 1976 when Brad Parks hit the first tennis ball from a wheelchair; the rest is history. The wheelchaired games today are an international sport, with 11 international tournaments and over 170 events. The qualifications are as follows:

A player must have a medically diagnosed permanent mobility related physical disability which must result in a substantial loss of function in one or both lower extremities.

An excellent place to obtain information on this activity that has opened new horizons to disabled people is to Google NEC Wheelchair Tennis Tours.

The social aspects of this sport are endless, ranging from playing on teams, to traveling to tennis matches of professionals locally and around the world, to having tennis parties while watching matches in the comfort of your home. The physical and social events of the sport can certainly add to the enjoyment and health of active senior citizens, and if one is so inclined, new doors to friendships can be explored that will keep one quite busy during retirement.

Sports – Golf

Most people who decide that they would like to give golf a try make the same mistakes that I did. I bought a 3 Wood (it was really made from titanium) for hitting the golf ball from the tee, a 7 iron for fairway shots, and an inexpensive putter for tapping the balls into practice holes. For the first couple of years, the only golf that I played was at various driving ranges in my neighborhood, except when I would carry the three pieces with me to vacation places around the country, always satisfied with hitting golf balls from tee areas on driving ranges and experimenting with my putter on practice greens. Well, what my method accomplished was that I picked up lots of bad habits from my experience at driving ranges that were exacerbated by the bad advice I received from other novice golfers. It wasn't until I began spending time in Florida, where my company had an office, that I decided that getting a set of golf clubs would be the next most logical next step in my learning experience. But, what brand of clubs should I buy? My golf buddies that had been playing the game for years all had their own preferences, such as Adams, Callaway, Cobra, Wilson, and a long list of other manufacturers. According to them, before buying an expensive set of clubs, certain considerations had to be addressed. My height and the size of my hands were very important as clubs that are too long or too short or handles that were too small or too big would reduce my efficiency and could possibly cause back, neck, arm, and leg injuries. After purchasing the **right clubs,** the **right balls** were the second most important part of the gear necessary in making me a champion golfer; the main choices seemed to be Top Flite, Titleist, or Maxifli. After selecting the right hardware, how I looked on the golf course seemed to be an important part of the game. So, wearing the right clothing became a hot topic of discussion between me and my friends. According to the "unwritten rules" of the game, shorts should be no more than two inches above the knees, with no bulging pockets. Short-sleeved shirts with no pockets and knitted collars, which make them lie flat and even, should also be part of the golf ensemble. Socks could be either short or long sweats, but must be white. Golf shoes should be white, or a combination of white and a limited number of other colors, preferably black or brown, and at all times should be spotlessly clean. Last but not least, the proper gloves should be worn so that when swinging at the golf ball the club remains in the holder's hands and not on the fairway. All of the above attire should be neutral in color so there is no distraction to other players; "No loud colors allowed."

Needless to say, speaking to my casual golf friends about their preferences became a dizzying experience as each had their own surefire method of playing the game. The best advice that I received was to hire a professional instructor and let him guide me through the fundamentals of the game, especially the rules, vocabulary, and the proper equipment that would suit my body and experience.

I purchased a book for beginners that discussed the vocabulary of the sport and many of its complex rules. An understanding of the vocabulary that is unique to the sport took quite a bit of time for me to learn, but eventually I got "into the swing of it." Some common words that should be memorized and understood before playing the game are:

- **Ace**......................is a hole in one. It's when the ball is hit from the tee and goes, one way or another, into a small targeted hole.
- **Eagle**.....................is two strokes under par.
- **Birdie**.....................is one stroke under par, which is the pre-designated standard score for the hole.
- **Par**........................is the pre-designated standard score or number of strokes given to each hole on the golf course.
- **Bogey**.....................is one stroke over par.
- **Bunker**....................is a sand trap or hazard.
- **Cart or Buggy**........is a small vehicle for transporting two players and their golf bags.
- **Chip**.......................is a low short shot to the green where the targeted hole resides.
- **Course**....................is a large area of land designed for playing golf.
- **Dog Leg**..................is a fairway that turns left or right.

- **Drive**......................is the first shot on every hole.
- **Driver**......................is the number 1 wood (which isn't made of wood but a variety of metals).
- **Driving Range**........is a practice area with mats or grass. Many ranges are designated for the use of irons or woods only.
- **Fairway**..................is part of the course between the tee and the green, which is kept free of rough grass.
- **Flag Stick**...............is the supporting flag on the green that is placed in the target hole.
- **Fore!**......................is the warning call when a ball is heading towards another player.
- **Green**......................is part of the golf course with grass cut very short, surrounding a hole. The hole contains a cup into which players try to "putt" their balls.
- **Handicap**...............is the numerical system of a golfer's playing ability, measured as under par or over par.
- **Hazard**...................is the difficulty or obstruction on golf courses such as lakes, ponds, fences, or bunkers (or sand traps).
- **Irons**......................are metal golf clubs numbered from 1 to 9.
- **Lie**..........................is the position in which the ball lies on the course.
- **Links**......................is a golf course beside the sea.
- **Mulligan**................is a second drive, where players grant each other a free stroke in a friendly game on the tee only. Mulligans are not officially permitted in professional play.
- **O.B.** .... is an abbreviation for "out of bounds" or beyond the limits of stakes or fences within the playing field.
- **Rough**....................is the area on the golf course where the grass is longer and thicker than on the fairway.
- **Scratch**...................a scratch player is one who has a "0" handicap and plays a par game.
- **Stroke or Shot**.......is the movement of the club when aimed at hitting the ball.

While learning the unique vocabulary of the sport, I read every book I could get my hands on about the rules of the game. There are basically two forms of play, one which is decided by the holes won and lost (match play), and the more popular form, which is decided by the total number of strokes taken to complete the round (stroke play). The primary rule is that the game is a gentlemen's sport and at all times the players must conduct themselves accordingly. The etiquette of the game covers both **Courtesy and Priority on the Course** as well as the **Care of the Course.** Some of the rules of the game are:

> **1-**Don't move, talk, or stand close to the player striking the ball.
> **2-**Don't play until the group in front of you is safely out of the way.
> **3-**Always play without delay and leave the putting green as soon as all the players in your group have holed out.
> **4-**Invite faster groups to play ahead of you (play through).
> **5-**Repair divots (holes) on fairway, and smooth footprints and disruptions in sand bunkers.
> **6-**Don't step on the line of another player's putt.
> **7-**Don't drop clubs on the putting green.
> **8-**Replace the flag stick carefully.

I was fortunate that my company maintained an office in Boca Raton, Florida. It gave me an opportunity to spend the months of January and February in the sun. We rented a townhouse at Pelican Harbor in Delray Beach, which was only a 10 minute ride to my office. We searched for a private place to play golf and settled for the Boca Country Club, where golf and tennis are the primary sports; they also allowed players that were not residents of their community to become members of the club. I was determined to take the advice of some of my friends to take the sport seriously and find a good golf instructor to undo many of the bad habits that I accumulated over the years, and hopefully learn the right way to play the game to the best of my ability.

I asked some of the better players in the club who they would recommend as a good coach; someone named Steve seemed to be the favorite instructor for most of them. So I asked Steve if he would consider taking me on as a student. He said he would like to see me hit some balls from the driving range to determine if I had the physical capacity for him to be interested in coaching me. On a clear windless day, we headed for the driving range, where he laid out six balls in a row for me. I had no trouble hitting them with my driver, but not one was straight; they were all over the place. I thought I was doomed, but he laid out another set of six and told me to step back and do some stretching; arms first, then hamstrings, then 20 soft practice swings. With that out of the way, he gave me my first lesson: "Always warm up before starting to swing." Then he corrected my grip, and I hit most of the balls dead center to the fairway. He told me that I had lots of bad habits that needed to be undone, but in time he thought that I would do just fine as a golfer. He told me to throw my clubs away and immediately go to the Golf Center to purchase a set of measured clubs. It was determined that Cobra offset clubs would do the trick. I was measured for arm length and club grip and told to return in a week to practice with the club's pro to see if the clubs were okay. The clubs were made from titanium, which made them light and easy to swing, which made my practice sessions fun and effective. My big question was, "When do I use the different clubs?" The answer was, "That depends on you and your experience, so practice and play often, then you'll know what each club will do in your hands."

At that point in time, I had all the proper attire, and with my new set of clubs I was ready to start playing the game in earnest. But as I learned when I began taking dancing seriously, "A new pair of dancing shoes doesn't mean that you know how to dance." I told Steve I would like to play in a game; he strongly suggested that I wait until at least six lessons and *mucho* practice before attempting to play, as playing badly at the beginning of a golf experience is one of the top reasons that many golfers give up the sport. So I took my six lessons and practiced every day after work and several hours on weekends. Soon, I knew which clubs to use and thought I was ready to play the game with some degree of success.

My first game was a nightmare; I played the game with my brains instead of my body, which resulted in my hitting the ball in every wrong direction possible. Steve was right; I played so badly that I almost gave up the sport. Steve suggested that we play a game together so he could see what was wrong. His first suggestion was to relax and not think of anything but the ball and where it should be headed. Relaxing seemed to be the key ingredient in my game; with him alongside me, my game improved considerably and helped me develop some confidence, which is another main ingredient to successfully play golf.

The club had a Senior Men's League, which Steve suggested I join. I was surprised to learn that I was the **kid on the block.** Most of the members were in their seventies and eighties; I was just in my sixties. The advantage that the older players had over me was that they knew the course very well and they were in no rush to finish their play. I got many pointers from my fellow golfers, which in time would allow me to play a game to my satisfaction. At that time, I was still a working person so I had to find time to play between my other responsibilities, but it laid the groundwork for my being comfortable with the sport when I retired several years later; it gave me something to look forward to with what developed into a passion for the game. The most important thing I learned was that there is no age limit in the sport. I played with members that were in their nineties—much to my embarrassment, as they beat me in my first year of play, every time. Our club also had a 9-hole league for players who were not able to complete an 18-hole game or didn't have the time or inclination required to play a longer game. One of the side advantages of playing golf for me was that our long yearly drives from New York to Florida were always planned around stops that had places for me to play my favorite game.

The Senior Club was responsible for our becoming welcomed guests at the club's social functions, and also for developing lasting relationships with other passionate golfers.

For those with access to computers, finding a place to play golf is as easy as typing in www.golfdigest.com or www.golflink.com. Each website displays information about locations, course profiles, course rules, and the cost to play. I use these sites to locate the courses that I would like to try when we travel down south in the winter. I usually call the facility and tell them when I'll be arriving so that they can set me up with a partner. While I'm playing, Barbara manages to locate places to shop, enjoying the quality time away from me while she indulges in her favorite pastime.

Golf, like tennis, is another sport that is intertwined with social activity. Making friends on the golf course is easy, especially if using a golf cart as it accommodates two people. When competing, there are usually two carts per team, with prizes for the ball closest to the hole from an initial drive, lowest overall score, best play on the difficult holes, and a number of other competitive prizes. The camaraderie and competiveness result in making numerous friends, all with a love for the sport. In addition, there are many social events that include dinners, dancing, and traveling with fellow golfers to vacations spots to play the game.

Boating

One way or another, we are all sports fans, whether as a participant, an avid fan whose enjoyment in life is attending sport functions, or as a couch television spectator. The lists of sporting activities are endless: golf, tennis, baseball, football, hockey, basketball, softball, fishing, boat racing, skiing, mountain climbing, log rolling, rodeo activity, car racing, and on and on. Of course, as we age and reach retirement, many of the above sports are no longer available or advisable on a participating basis. But being an avid fan or sedentary onlooker are certainly realistic activities in our senior years. Barbara and I were lucky in that we were active boaters in our younger days and were able to continue enjoying that activity well into our retirement years.

One of our retirement dreams was to spend a month on our 42-foot Chris-Craft and cruise, if possible, to Montauk Point, Long Island; Block Island, Rhode Island; then on to Massachusetts enjoying stops at Martha's Vineyard, Nantucket, Cape Cod, and then sailing through Buzzard's Bay to New Bedford and up the Cape Cod Canal to Plymouth. After completing that semicircle, we would then head for our favorite port, Newport, Rhode Island for an extended stay and finally back to our homeport in Greenport, Long Island. What a wonderful dream come true that trip would be. To appreciate where our passion for boating comes from, a little of our history with boats is in order.

We bought our first boat, a new 18-foot Crestliner runabout, two years after we were married with money we had saved to take a two-week vacation in Italy. We had even taken courses in Italian at Brooklyn College to prepare for our first *Bucket List* trip. We had saved $2,500 and were ready, willing, and able to board a jet plane and fly to our new adventure. But fate intervened through my father-in-law Charley, who surprised us with tickets to the New York Boat Show at the Coliseum in Manhattan. We were excited to visit the show as we were slowly becoming avid sailors, thanks to my father-in-law and his 28-foot fishing boat, which we had been guests on almost every weekend during the past two summers. Bypassing the mega yachts, cruisers, houseboats, and sailboats, we stopped and fell in love with an 18-foot Crestliner that was driven by a 60HP outboard Johnson motor; the price was $2,500. It didn't take long for us to decide that having a boat was an ongoing vacation and that a trip to Italy was a great idea but could be postponed for another time. So we put our vacation to Italy back on our *Bucket List*, and purchased a new 1966 Crestliner. We named our new princess *Big One* because of its small size, and knowing that someday in the future we would own a "*Bigger One*."

The first thing we had to do was take some boating safety courses; our choice was either the United States Coast Guard Auxiliary or a private organization, the United States Power Squadron (USPS). As I had already spent four years in the United States Air Force, joining an organization connected with the Coast Guard was not an attractive option for me; so we both joined the USPS and took our first safe boating course in Seamanship. Some history about the USPS is in order to understand the importance of that non-profit organization and its impact on boating safety, and how joining such an organization can fit in nicely into one's retirement years as the social networking in the organization are endless:

USPS was founded in 1914 and currently has over 45,000 members in 450 squadrons throughout the United States. Its main purpose is teaching mariners the importance of safe boating through education. The levels of courses are: Seamanship, Piloting, Plotting and Position Finding, Celestial Navigation, Cruise Planning, Engine Maintenance, Marine Electronics, Sailing, and much more. In addition to the intellectual endeavors of the organization, there is also an active social side. It is a fraternal group that encourages participation in on-the-water and on-land activities, such as cruising, boat rendezvous, sail races, navigation contests, and even fishing derbies. Activities ashore include meetings with marine programs and teaching classes, parties, dinner dances, picnics, field trips, and an annual Change of Watch Ball.

We took our Seamanship course at Saint Francis College in Brooklyn, NY. We both passed the course in 1966; I was sworn in and became a member of the Brooklyn Power Squadron. Not so for Barbara, even though she took the same course and passed the same tests (with higher grades than me). At that time, women were not allowed to become members; it wouldn't be until 1984 that she would become a full member with the same standing as *moi*, even though she was sworn in alongside me and probably became the first woman to be sworn into the USPS. What we noticed at the meetings and dinners that we attended were the advanced ages of many of the bridge members. Many of them had been members for over 20 years and had made the organization a major part of their lives. Barbara and I decided that the USPS would certainly be a great way to remain active in something we loved through our adult years and into retirement. What better way to spend our retirement than to be involved with a fraternal group whose main purpose is having fun while boating safely? We currently are members of the Peconic Power Squadron of Long Island and keep active with their safe boating programs and many social events.

Big One was part of our family for seven years. One of our boating friends had a 26-foot Chris-Craft cruiser named *Paper Doll* that we fell in love with after spending a day fishing aboard the beamy beauty. Barbara and I decided that it would be the perfect boat for us, being that the runabout was getting a little crowded for our growing family of four. *Paper Doll* had double bunks and could easily accommodate our two small children, Steve and Laurie, who were four and three years old at that time. In addition, it had a somewhat private V-berth at the bow of the boat for Barbara and me, which added up to a boat we could all sleep on and spend some quality time together after my grueling tax seasons as an accountant, which, for all intents and purposes, ended for me on the first of April each year.

So the admiral (Barbara) sent me to Al Grover's Chris-Craft

dealership in Freeport, Long Island, which at that time was the pleasure boating capital of New York, to find our next dream boat. He had just the boat we were looking for and it was only a few years old. I gave him a deposit, but before we signed the contract, Al said, "Wait, I have a 1970, two-year-old, 28-foot Chris-Craft that was just traded and I think you should have a look at her; she is a beauty." Well, one look was all it took. The boat was much larger overall than the 26-footer; it's surprising how much difference two feet makes in a boat. It had lots of headroom, a nice kitchenette, a standup toilet, double bunk beds for the kids that folded down into a couch, and a nice size V-berth at the bow. What more can a soul need? The boat was $500 more than the smaller craft. I didn't waste any time in making her a member of our family by signing on the "dotted line." When I got home and told Barbara that I had bought a larger boat, she went into shock. She didn't expect me to purchase anything without her first seeing it and was annoyed that I went over our budget. All of her displeasure faded away when she boarded our new purchase, *Alice B*, which was the name on the transom of the boat that was meticulously painted royal blue by its previous owner. Being that I went over budget, we decided not to spend any additional funds changing the name on the craft. Barbara immediately fell in love with the beautiful lady. Its shiny powder-blue fiberglass hull, with a white wood superstructure, a single 225HP inboard engine, a private standup toilet, a freshwater pump system, and a propane gas stove, was a far cry from what she expected after being cramped in a smaller boat for so many years. She told me from that time on I could buy any boat without asking her as she knew that it would be a perfect addition to our family. We would joke a lot about the name of the boat. As long as we owned *Alice B*, people that we met while cruising called my wife Barbara, Alice; we made a point of never correcting anyone right away and got many laughs when we explained later that Alice was not my wife's name.

As time went by, our kids outgrew their upper and lower bunks, so we looked around for our third boat and fell in love once more (how fickle we were) with a 35-foot all-fiberglass Chris-Craft Double Cabin cruiser. We were lucky to find the exact boat that we wanted: a two-year-old 1977 35-foot Chris-Craft Double Cabin. It was a whole different kind of boat than our previous ones. It had twin 300HP engines, a 5KW generator, a toilet with a standup shower, a heat and air conditioning pump, a private master bedroom, a V-berth for Laurie with a privacy door, and a folding bed for Steve. After a family meeting, we decided to call our new family member *"Mikara,"* which is derived from the first three letters of Mike and the last three letters of Barbara. It is also sort of a play on words with the Italian word *"Mikara,"* which means, in dialect, "my love."

With the availability of "LORAN C" for pleasure boats as a direction finder, we didn't waste any time in purchasing the electronic battery-operated system and putting it to good use. With its help as a navigation aide, we took our first trip on our 35-foot beauty from Long Island, NY to Plymouth, MA. What a pleasure it was to travel and arrive at planned destinations without zigzagging or getting lost. After ten wonderful boating years, we decided it was time to buy our last boat, which we planned to live on permanently when we retired, while traveling throughout the United States and the islands off of Florida.

We currently own our second *Mikara* and recently celebrated her 25th anniversary as a family member. She is a 1988 47-foot Chris-Craft, measured from bow rail to swim platform, has two 450HP engines, a 7KW generator, a master bedroom with a private head (toilet) with a nice size tub, a private guest room with a head, a full size refrigerator, a kitchen, a living room (salon), heat and air conditioning, and all of the latest electronic entertainment toys. On the bridge, we have radar, GPS, auto pilot, and a multitude of radios. It's just the right boat to have in our retirement years for traveling, and enjoying the sun at home and in faraway places. A photo of *Mikara* with Admiral Barbara at the bow and me at the helm follows:

We have kept our boats at Stirling Harbor Marina, on the North Fork of Long Island in the seaport Village of Greenport for over 30 years, and consider it our home away from home in the summer months. We chose the location after spending time in the Hamptons, on the South Fork, because it was much lower keyed than its southern sister. The water in the area is deep compared to the South Shore, which makes boating a lot safer and more relaxing. It's also one of the best jumping-off points for boating on the East Coast, putting Connecticut, Rhode Island, Massachusetts, and Maine within reasonable boating distances. Cruising to Connecticut, Block Island, or Sag Harbor for lunch are some of our favorite short trips from our convenient homeport.

What attracted us to the quaint town of Greenport was the laid back attitude of its townspeople, and the farmers that could be seen around town wearing their blue, shoulder strap coveralls. It also didn't have the crowded restaurants and traffic jams that the popular Hamptons on the South Fork is noted for. In addition, the inland boating waterways were less crowded and its islands, from a distance, reminded us of the friendly islands of the Mediterranean. We were always amazed that on some days the only boats to be seen were at a distance, which is very unusual for a popular seafaring area.

The town itself has a rather checkered history, ranging from whaling, shipbuilding, rum running, and illegal whiskey trading to fishing and oyster harvesting. It was also home of the America's Cup winners, *Enterprise* in 1930, *Rainbow* in 1934, and *Ranger* in 1937. Its history has made the village the quaint but sophisticated town that it is today. Needless to say, it no longer participates in any of the above illegal activities.

The focal point of the village today is Mitchell Park, which became fully operational in 2007. Its main attraction is an Antique Carousel that was built in 1920 by the Herschell-Spillman Company and donated to the town by the Northrop/Grumman Corporation in 1995. It is fully enclosed in a glass pavilion and boasts of having one of the few brass ring dispensers in use today. Its hours during the season are from 10:00 AM to 9:00 PM. These same hours apply on weekends and holidays during the off season, weather permitting. The park's amphitheater is connected to a harbor walk and is the site for band concerts, theatrical shows, and special local events. Its harbor walk connects the park to the Long Island Railroad Station, which travels to New York City, and also connects with the North Ferry, which carries cars and passengers across the narrow body of water in Greenport Harbor to Shelter Island. The park also has an ice-skating rink for outdoor winter sports, which is used as a mist walk in the summer months to cool the area. Its *Camera Obscura* is a medieval optical device that projects a live image from outside to a round projection table in its dark room, and is one of the only projections in the world that is open to the public free of charge. The park also has a harbormaster's building, observation deck, public toilets, and over 80 transient town boat slips.

Of special interest to us are the musical events that take place at the amphitheater during summer months. Once a week, the residents bring their chairs and sit on the expansive lawn outside the theater to enjoy the Greenport Band, which is made up of approximately twenty local musicians, playing popular and marching music. Dancing bands are also scheduled throughout the season playing Dixieland, Jazz, Smooth, and hot Latin music. Our last dance session was to the music of the Mambo Loco Quartet of Brentwood, Long Island, which is considered one of the hottest bands on the Twin Forks.

Our dream of spending a month on *Mikara* cruising at our leisure had finally become a reality. We had our nautical charts out and began plotting courses to the faraway places we'd dreamt of visiting with no restrictions as to how long to remain in each place. We were retired and the world was our oyster! The best time to travel along the eastern seaboard is in the middle of July when the seas are calm and rain and fog are less prevalent. But, there are no guarantees that traveling that time of year won't get a sailor in trouble with inclement weather. So it becomes difficult making reservations at planned ports-of-call, without saying a prayer or two. Reservations are required at popular marinas months in advance to secure docking space, even though cruising is totally reliant on weather conditions during planned vacations. There are many foolish sailors who will travel under any conditions and, somehow, live to tell of their ordeals as if they were gallant adventures.

It's possible to plan a stay at a marina for two days and remain for a week, due to unexpected inclement weather conditions. But, if a person loves boating, as we do, they will throw caution to the wind, so to speak, and make early reservations in anticipation that the weather gods will cooperate. For our first extended vacation, we made reservations at Montauk Yacht Club, in Montauk, Long Island; then on to Champlin's Marina in Block Island, Rhode Island; then to the town dock at Menemsha, on Martha's Vineyard, Massachusetts, with our next stops in the same state to Nantucket Boat Basin, in Nantucket, and then to Hyannis, in Cape Cod. Leaving the "Bean State," we planned on cruising to Newport, Rhode Island for an extended period of time or until we tired of the place—if that's possible, considering the incredible number of places to explore and its wonderful beaches.

Discussing the many wonderful places we visited would take volumes, so I'll just write about one of our trips to the Cape Cod, MA and the Newport, RI areas, which was at the time of the JFK Jr's plane crash on July 16, 1999, that killed him, his wife Carolyn Bessette, and her sister Lauren.

After leaving our home port in Greenport, Long Island, we visited Montauk Point which is located on the South Fork of Long Island. After spending a few days on the point of Long Island, enjoying the beautiful beaches and its quaint town, we headed for Block Island, Rhode Island, where we spent three days enjoying the cool breezes that visit the island, the sun, their pristine beaches, and of course, their first class restaurants. We left Block Island for Martha's Vineyard, which was our next port-of-call, and were told by the Harbor Master of the island, who we contacted by short-wave-radio, that the area was under surveillance by naval vessels and helicopters and that we would have to bypass it because JFK, Jr. and his wife and her sister were presumed to have crashed in his single engine plane in the vicinity. We headed for our next destination, the island of Nantucket in Massachusetts, which was approximately 80 miles from Block Island. If we were lucky and had good weather with no unforeseen mishaps, it would take about five to six hours to reach the "The Grey Lady," which got its name due to the dense fog that visits the island so frequently.

The NOAA weather forecast was pretty good for the day, so we were off on the next leg of our trip by 10:00 AM. The body of water that we were traveling can be very tricky as currents from several different directions meet along the route to Vineyard and Nantucket Sounds. The strong currents from Buzzards Bay can cause some large broadside waves on the port (left) side of the boat, or the Atlantic Ocean's currents can cause some pretty big swells on the starboard (right) side of the vessel. While approaching Menemsha Bight in Martha's Vineyard, which was our original destination, we spotted some debris in the water that looked strange and could possibly have been from John's missing plane. We immediately called the Coast Guard and gave them our latitude and longitude positions so they could locate and investigate the scene; they thanked us and before the conversation was over a search vessel was at the site.

Unfortunately, it was debris from the aircraft, which sent us into a depressed state, causing Barbara to cry uncontrollably. We moved from the area slowly and had to do some tricky maneuvering to get past all the naval vessels in the water around the island. We called Nantucket Boat Basin and spoke to the dock master, George, whom we have known for many years, and explained our circumstances, hoping he would have an empty boat slip for us. He said, "Come on in. Very few people have been able to move their boats because of the restricted area around the accident." We were delighted and relieved that he had a berth available for us. It prevented our having to make an unexpected stop in Cape Cod, which meant we would then have to cross over to Nantucket and back to the Cape again, passing some pretty nasty shallow water, especially dangerous when pea soup (fog) is present.

The currents were very strong as we approached Nantucket Sound; luckily for us, they were coming from behind us and pushed *Mikara* to a cruising speed of 22 mph, which we had never achieved at 3,400 rpm. It usually takes the engines about 4,000 rpm for her to move that fast. We got to Nantucket much sooner than anticipated, just in time to avoid the strong winds that are so prevalent in the early afternoons from the Atlantic Ocean, which were just starting to pick up. There is a very narrow inlet at the entrance to Nantucket, so it's imperative that boats entering stay on the right side of the channel, especially if ferries or large commercial vessels are exiting. Once past the channel, Nantucket Boat Basin's bulk-headed marina is immediately apparent on the right side of the harbor.

Waiting for permission to enter the marina from the dock master George is always tricky, especially when the wind starts to kick up, as it did. *Mikara* has a tendency to be pushed away from the entrance of the protected area when it gets windy, so getting behind the bulk-headed sea walls took some nifty maneuvering. George gave us our docking assignment on our VHF radio. I throttled up to get to the marina's entrance, but had to immediately throttle down upon entering as the steering area is very narrow and winding, with boats docked on all sides. After zigzagging past the boats that were securely tied to their docks, I finally reached my slip and backed in with the help of the prevailing strong winds. It was a long and tedious trip, and we were glad to be secure at such a pristine and boater-friendly facility. We had been going to this marina for over 15 years and were always thrilled when tying *Mikara* up at our temporary home. This year was special because we had no deadline as to when we had to leave; we were retired and decided that we would leave whenever the weather and the "call-to-the-next-port" beckoned us. The marina is located at the end of the town, which makes for a picturesque view when looking from the town at the marina or from the marina at the beautifully landscaped town. *The Waterway Guide*, Northern edition, describes the marina perfectly:

> Nantucket Boat Basin sets an industry standard for service at its transient marina. You will find 243 slips to accommodate boats from 30 to 280 feet in length, as well as dockside electricity, water, fuel, ice, public phones, and waste disposal, with individualized pump-out stations designed to reach virtually every slip. Ashore are restrooms and showers, a large 24/7 coin-operated laundry, rental cottages, rustic artists' studios along the wharves, and even a park for pets' needs. The Boat Basin concierge, whose headquarters is located at the fuel dock, can arrange restaurant reservations, sightseeing trips, car rentals, medical appointments, and babysitting services.

Well, I guess that just about says it all for this spotless marina whose staff is professional and boasts of having the world's most polite, experienced dock boys and girls to accommodate their guests' every wish.

Nantucket Island is one of the most natural and beautiful islands that I have ever had the pleasure of visiting. It has its own idyllic persona, derived from its beaches and the abundance of beautifully landscaped designed and natural wild flowers. The island is only three and a half miles from north to south and is 14 miles long, with miles of clean, well-maintained beaches. It's rich with fields of Scotch broom, bayberries, beach plum, grapes, bearberries, and hundreds of varieties of wildflowers. Its Milestone Road cranberry bog is one of the largest on the East Coast and its aromatic flavor seems to capture the air that flows throughout the island. We have seen deer, pheasants, cottontail rabbits, and all kinds of birds on our walks around the island. As a bonus from nature, Harbor seals are seen year round, sunbathing and playing off the beaches. Whale watching is still viable by sightseeing boats that guarantee sighting them on every excursion. One of the island's biggest tourist attractions is biking; people travel from all over the country with their bikes, crossing over on one of the many ferries from the mainland, and spend days biking and camping on the many excellent paths throughout one of nature's few remnants of paradise remaining on the East Coast.

Some years ago, our son Steve and his wife Donna joined us on the island after crossing over on one of the ferries from Cape Cod, with their bikes, ready to explore the unique island. We thought we would spend some quality time with them, but lost them for most of their visit to the "Call of the Wild," beautiful Nantucket. On each of their excursions, Donna would gather wildflowers and return to *Mikara* with them. By the time they left the island, our boat looked like a florist's shop with flowers decorating our bridge, deck, salon, and bedrooms. Biking is one of the most popular methods of transportation on the island; cars are discouraged and must pay exorbitant fees to cross over on the ferries, but there are many auto rentals on the island at relatively reasonable rates. Taxis are an alternative if other transportation is not available, but the shuttle bus system is the most efficient and affordable method of getting around if biking isn't feasible. The Nantucket Regional Transit Authority (NRTA) provides an island-wide seasonal fixed-rate shuttle service and a year-round "Your Island Ride" van service. In season, the shuttle buses run every 15 minutes from the center of the town and circle the island. The fares are reasonable, from $1.00 to $2.00 each way, with discounts for senior citizens and no charge for children under six. Our favorite method of transportation is by foot, as walking around the island can be a pleasant way to spend the day, if the temperature is in the low 80s. When it gets near 90 degrees, we prefer the convenient shuttle buses.

We kept tuned to the radio to get up-to-date information on the rescue ships; the bodies still were not found, but additional wreckage had been located. I'm sure the debris that we alerted the Coast Guard to was a part of that recovery, but nothing significant had been uncovered about the passengers of the ill-fated plane.

We decided to take advantage of the cool weather of about 80 degrees, and walk around the island, ending our journey at the Nantucket Memorial Airport, which was the fictitious setting for the television sit-com *Wings*. But as the great Scottish poet, Robert Burns, wrote: "The best laid plans of mice and men gang aft agley," our journey didn't go exactly as planned, as we had a few unexpected surprises on our way to the airport. We mapped our walkathon carefully, beginning at the cobblestone streets outside our marina. The streets are inhabited by surprising colonial, Georgian, and Greek revival houses of ship's captains and whaling merchants, dating back to the 18th century and are still intact. Many of the houses have engraved plates that identify the dates they were built and the original occupants' names. We stopped at the Nantucket Whaling and Life-Saving Museums, which gave us some insight and a better understanding of the dangers that the mariners faced at a time when they had to go to sea to survive, but didn't always return home due to the hazardous nature of the elements and their dangerous encounters with the giant whales.

To appreciate the importance of whaling on the lives of these brave seamen, some history of Nantucket is necessary. It wasn't until 1602 that Captain Bartholomew Gosnold of Falmouth, England, sailed his bark *Concord* past the bluff of Siasconset and mapped out the territory for dear old England. The 2,500 native Americans living in peace on the island were the Wampanoag Indians; they called their home *Nantican, Natocke,* or *Naytucan,* which is thought to mean "Far away island" or "In the midst of waters." The island was deeded to Thomas Mayhew by the English Crown in 1641. Up until that time, Indians from Cape Cod and Martha's Vineyard sought refuge on Nantucket from the European interlopers and consolidated their energy and skills with the local natives to fish and harvest the whales that washed up on the shore. The Europeans didn't settle on the island until 1659, when Mayhew sold his interest to the "Nine original purchasers," for 30 English pounds and two beaver hats, one for himself and the other for his wife. English ingenuity brought whaling offshore and, with the help and skill of the Native Americans, Nantucket became the world's leading whaling port from the mid-17th to the early 18th centuries. Prior to the colonials' invasion, the natives harvested Drift and Right whales that were near the shore or were washed up on the beaches. The whales were 30 to 60 feet in length and weighed upwards of 60 tons. The English readily saw that a profit could be made by commercializing whale hunting. Whale oil for lamps and whalebone and ivory for ladies' corsets, buggy whips, parasol ribs, and scrimshaw proved to be a rainmaker and the main industry of the island.

Walking along the bustling cobblestone, three-block town, we stopped and browsed antique galleries specializing in scrimshaw, China trade porcelain, old hooked rugs, country furniture, weathervanes, English antiques, and maritime artifacts. The most fascinating items sold in many of the upscale stores were whale ivory lightship pocketbook-baskets, which were decorated with nautical scrimshaw created by sailors of bygone days and lightship attendants. The starting prices of these begin at around $800 and can cost into the tens of thousands of dollars if they are very old and designed by famous artists. Today, it is illegal to use whalebones or ivory for artistic purposes, so these original baskets keep increasing in value. It's amusing to see many ladies walking around town with these baskets hanging from their arms, as if they were showing off trophies or badges of honor. I bought a miniature one decorated with a plastic design of a whale for my Xmas tree that cost 50 bucks and proudly hang it on my seven-foot artificial tree annually, with a smile and chuckle, as I picture the expensive baskets dangling from proud Nantucket ladies' arms.

During the summer season, the population of the island reaches 50,000-plus people from its year-round residency of 10,000. The influx of tourists and summer residents keeps the island's commercial establishment busy and the town's streets crowded, so it was a relief to head out of town away from the crowds to our final location for the day, the Nantucket Memorial Airport, which was located a little over three miles from the center of the town. I was wearing comfortable sneakers, but my feet were killing me from walking on the town's cobblestone pavement. It was also close to noon, and the sun was starting to throw off more heat than we expected. But we were retired and had all the time in the world to walk and explore the roads leading up to the airport. So we headed south on Orange Street toward Gardener Court and walked a mile to the traffic circle. That is where we got into trouble.

We stopped and asked a woman in a coffee shop how far it was to the airport. She said "Just a few minutes up the road." So we purchased some large cold soft drinks, which we desperately needed as we were both getting weary from walking on the uneven roads and from the temperature that was rising to the upper 80s. We began our "Few minutes' walk" and couldn't fathom why we weren't reaching our destination in that period of time. Well, evidently the lady we asked for directions thought we were traveling by car and her "Few minutes" was in motorized time, not walking time. The two-mile walk took forever; we were sweating out of control and our feet were literally on fire. There was absolutely no place along the road to take shelter and when we finally reached the airport, I was tempted to run to it for shelter, but lacked the energy to do so.

We were facing the entrance to a three-runway airport, expecting to see some resemblance to the fictional Tom Never Field in the popular television sit-com *Wings* that ran from 1990 to 1997, but there was none. The show was one of our favorites; it was about the Hackett brothers, Joe and Brian, played by Timothy Daly and Steven Weber, who were pilots and operated Sandpiper Airline from Nantucket's only airport. Mr. Daly played a highly responsible but mildly neurotic and compulsively neat pilot who owned the one-plane Sandpiper Airline. He originally planned to launch the airline with Carol, his fiancée, who worked behind the ticket counter, but his brother Brian ran off with her, causing a falling out between the brothers that lasted throughout the comedy's long TV run. Other cast members were Tony Shalhoub, of TV's *Monk* fame, as an oddball cab driver, and Crystal Bernard as the on-again, off-again girlfriend.

We rushed into the air-conditioned waiting room and almost collapsed with delight from the refreshing cold air caressing our overheated, sweaty bodies. The inside of the airport was a facsimile of the one in the sit-com, so we were immediately at home with sitting on the small cafeteria counter seats and ordering extra-large glasses of water to cool us off and large ice cream sodas to make sure our bodies would pleasantly recover from our uncomfortable walkathon. We decided, then and there, that in the future we would either ride bikes or take the shuttle bus or a taxicab for any walking distance of over one mile. Accordingly, we called a cab to take us back to *Mikara,* which took all of 15 air-conditioned refreshing minutes. When we arrived at our boat, we immediately showered to cool down and then turned on the radio to see if there were any new developments about John-John's plan crash; there was no new information.

We put on our bathing suits and walked a couple of blocks to the beach, where we spent the rest of the bright day under an umbrella hiding from the sun, and soaking in the refreshing salt water. After our beach excursion, we picked up some take-out food from one of the seafood restaurants on the wharf, went back to *Mikara,* unpacked, and devoured our meals, with lots of cold water, watched some TV, and literally passed out from the day's exhausting experience.

The first thing the next morning we turned on our TV for an update of the naval search. Additional ships with sophisticated sensors had arrived and gathered offshore to continue probing for any wreckage of the fallen aircraft. Investigators released new data that portrayed the final half minute of Jr.'s doomed flight as an **"UNCONTROLLED PLUNGE INTO THE SEA."** Although we expected that news, we were greatly saddened by the event and decided to do some sightseeing as a distraction.

As we dined at the "Brotherhood of Thieves" restaurant we learned a particular piece of American history that tweaked our curiosity, especially Barbara's, as she is an avid amateur stargazer. Maria (pronounced Ma-RYE-ah) Mitchell, astronomer, librarian, and 19th century intellectual, first cousin to Benjamin Franklin, four times removed, was born on the island in 1818. She earned international fame and was awarded a gold medal from the King of Denmark for discovering a telescopic comet. The discovery resulted in her being the first woman elected to a fellowship in the American Academy of Arts and Science, and she was the first woman Professor of Astronomy in the United States. She also promoted women's suffrage and higher education and, as President of the American Association for the Advancement of Women, she was able to forward her beliefs with authority. We headed straight for the Maria Mitchell Observatory and Museum to learn more about this incredible lady who also discovered that sunspots are whirling vertical cavities and not clouds, as previously thought.

We were surprised to see about 50 children, ranging from 10 to 15 years of age, attending celestial demonstrations at the observatory. We joined in one of the classes and learned how to observe the sun by making a hole in a piece of paper and allowing the sun to shine through and reflect onto a table. We joined another tour and explored a scale model of the solar system, a planar sundial, and even observed sunspots. Barbara couldn't wait to climb the ladder to an old telescope and sample some of the daylight sights in the distant sky. She was determined to return in the evening, time permitting, to further explore the solar system. We spent the remaining week on the island playing golf, swimming at several of the beaches, eating lunch and dinner at rustic restaurants, and socializing with our boating friends and the friendly people of Nantucket.

We were excited that our last evening in Nantucket would include enjoying the music of the Boston Pops Orchestra's "Great Social" that was to be performed at Jetties Beach, which was adjacent to our marina. We left a half hour before the scheduled performance with our beach chairs and walked the short distance so we could find a good seating location; the beach was already crowded, so we had to settle for a spot that was quite a distance from the bandstand. We got comfortable and then applied anti-mosquito lotion to all the exposed parts of our bodies to avoid becoming the flying cannibals' evening BBQs. The program indicated that, during and after the concert, there would be fireworks by the world-renowned firm of Grucci (officially called Pyrotechnique by Grucci, Inc.). The theme for the evening was "A Dedication to the Music of John Williams," conducted by the man himself. He is considered the most prolific writers in the history of movie music and probably one of the most widely heard composers of the 20th and 21st centuries. His awards for music compositions are endless; he is the recipient of five Academy Awards, four Golden Globes, seven BAFTA Awards (British Academy of Film and Television Arts), and ten Grammy Awards. He was inducted into the Hollywood Bowl Hall of Fame in the year 2000 and was the recipient of the Kennedy Center's Honors in 2004. Some of his movie compositions were in *Schindler's List*, the six *Star Wars* films of George Lucas, Steven Spielberg's *Raiders of the Lost Ark*, the other *Indiana Jones* movies, *Jaws*, *Jurassic Park*, *Superman*, and numerous other movies and TV scores. The native Long Islander (born in Floral Park) was the conductor of the Boston Pops Orchestra from 1980 until 1993, and also has been a guest conductor at venues throughout the world during his illustrious career.

The orchestra played many of his compositions from famous movies and TV shows while the Grucci team displayed their expertise in producing state-of-the-art, spectacular fireworks. The evening ended with the orchestra playing "God Bless America" as the crowd of thousands joined in singing the beautiful lyrics. This was complemented by an incredible display of firework replicas of the American flag and atomic bomb-like explosions. Multi-colored flares decorated and illuminated the sky, and their sonic sounds and vibrations shook the surrounding beach front, which made the hair on the back of my neck stand straight up from the noise and the feeling of pride in singing one of our nation's sacred patriotic songs.

On our way back to *Mikara,* we stopped for a nightcap at one of the restaurants that had a panoramic view of the harbor and shared its docks with our marina. We were still concerned about the JFK, Jr. crash and we were feeling sort of spooked at the prospect of crossing from Nantucket to Hyannis, Cape Cod, which happened to be where the Kennedy Family Compound is located, because of the ever-present fog that seems to engulf the preferred traveling route across the Sound. We returned to our resting place and reviewed our charts, carefully highlighting any possible dangerous areas that might have rocks or shallow water. We decided that we should leave a little later than usual to give any morning fog a chance to burn off from the sun's rays.

In the morning, we received news that John-John's plane and its occupants had been recovered. This upset us to no end, considering we were about to travel the same general route of the crash. I said a silent prayer for them, and then remembered that in the area we were traveling there had also been a major ship collision between Italy's pride and joy cruise ship, *SS Andrea Doria* and the *MS Stockholm,* a smaller passenger liner of the Swedish American Line. On the *Andrea Doria's* 100th Atlantic crossing, it collided with, or to be more precise, was rammed on its right side by, the *Stockholm.* On that fateful day, July 25, 1956, the *Andrea Doria* was heading west passing the shores of

Nantucket on its voyage to New York, while the *Stockholm* was heading from New York, eastward toward the Nantucket Lighthouse, and then continuing across the North Atlantic Ocean to Sweden. The Italian liner had about 1,200 passengers and 500 crew members; the *Stockholm* had over 600 passengers including crew members. Deaths due to the infamous maritime collision were 46 on the Italian liner and 5 on the Swedish-American ship.

What happened? What caused the horrific collision that sank *Andrea Doria* the next day? It all boiled down to **"POOR VISIBILITY AND CARELESS SEAMANSHIP."** The Italian liner was traveling at about 25 mph while the *Stockholm* was cruising at about 20 mph in dense fog. Both ships saw each other on their respective radar screens, but neither attempted radio communication with the other. The *Stockholm* followed the "International Rules of the Road" and steered to the right to avoid collision; the *Andrea Doria* mistakenly steered to the left, bringing the right side of the ship directly in front of the *Stockholm*. Neither reduced their speed, which is customary when cruising in fog, and only slowed down after impact. In addition to the fatalities, hundreds were injured during the impact and the subsequent evacuation rescue, but fortunately, due to improved communication methods, and the fact that they were on a busy sea lane, which allowed nearby ships to respond to their distress calls quickly, most of the passengers avoided the horrific destiny of the 1,512 passengers on the *Titanic* in 1912 when it hit an iceberg while traveling **at night at high speeds;** even though they were forewarned that icebergs were in the vicinity of their route **(poor seamanship).**

One would think that after so many accidents that were caused by **poor seamanship** that we would have better failsafe systems in place on vessels. Even today, in the month of May, 2013, after so many unnecessary ship disasters that were caused by careless seamen, we have the Italian cruise ship *Costa Concordia* that is still capsized, as of this writing, after running aground on January 13, 2012 at the Isola del Giglio, Tuscany, Italy, in the Mediterranean Sea, because the Captain wanted to show off his beautiful 952 foot, 4,250 passenger ship to the islanders and carelessly ventured into unchartered shallow water, hitting and remaining on an underwater reef. Looking at pictures of the ship, which is about 1/3 under less than 26 feet of water and lying on its side, is bizarre because the reality of sailing vessels is that they float on top of the water upright. Again, **Poor Seamanship** caused the unnecessary death of 34 passengers and injury to over 300 others. The captain was arrested and charged with multiple manslaughter, failing to assist over 300 incapacitated passengers, failing to be the last one to leave the ship, and failing to describe to maritime authorities the scope of the disaster.

How similar was the JFK, Jr. incident to the above accidents? He was traveling at night with poor visibility, and, although his GPS was on, his autopilot was off. If it were on, it would have kept his plane on course and upright, giving him an opportunity to safely follow an electronic heading. Again, **"POOR VISIBILITY AND CARELESS SEAMANSHIP" caused an avoidable misfortune to become an unfortunate reality.** The air tower at Nantucket's airport stated that, seconds before the crash, his plane veered to the right and then suddenly went nose first into the sea. The technical information that was gathered after retrieving the wreckage of the plane, unfortunately, resulted in a lawsuit for negligence between the Bessette family and the estate of JFK, Jr. The case was settled out of court for the benefit of the plaintiff, without prolonged publicity, but it didn't discount the fact that he was not an experienced pilot when it came to flying under adverse weather conditions or at night.

We traveled across the sound to Hyannis, where we spent a week visiting the towns of Falmouth, Sandwich, Mashpee, Yarmouth, Denis, Chatham, and Providence (Pee town). We also visited the Denis Cape Playhouse Theatre, which is known as the "Birthplace of Stars," and is the oldest professional summer theatre in the United States. It boasts of having such illustrious actors as Bette Davis, Humphrey Bogart, Gregory Peck, and Ginger Rogers, among the many other renowned performers. We always make it a point to visit the Hyannis Melody Tent that seats up to 3,000 people and has a history of having the best entertainment on the Cape with such stars as Bill Cosby, Dolly Parton, Tony Bennett, and Jonny Lang.

Our last port-of-call was Newport, Rhode Island, which was approximately a six hour trip from the Cape. We spent a week exploring the mansions of the rich and famous of the 19th and early 20th centuries, such as, the Vanderbilt's 65,000 sq. ft. Breakers, the Astor's 17,000 sq. ft. Beachwood, Doris Duke's 49,000 sq. ft. Rough Point, and our favorite, the Hammersmith Farm, which was the childhood home of Jackie Bouvier Kennedy. Another favorite of ours was the "Newport Classical Music Festival," which is held annually for two weeks at many of the Newport Mansions, such as the Vanderbilt's Breakers and the E.J. Berwind's Elms.

Our week came to an abrupt end when we realized that our one-month dream vacation was over; so we prepared *Mikara* for her voyage back to Greenport and prayed for calm seas and clear skies, so we could complete our circular trip back to our home port. Our dream vacation on our boat had become a reality; what we hadn't realized was that spending extended periods of time in our confined home was not as wonderful as we thought it would be, and that traveling to Florida and down to the Bahamas on *Mikara* was something we decided we might leave for another lifetime.

What is interesting and so important when deciding what activities are right for you are the social aspects of the activities that are available in the chosen fields. In boating, there are social gatherings with the United States Power Squadron; there is lots of traveling, usually with companion boats, and entertainment becomes available that would otherwise be difficult to attain, such as the music festivals and beach fireworks. There is, without a doubt, an opportunity to meet new friends and develop lifetime relationships, which becomes so important in our golden years as these expand our interests and keep adding to our physical as well as our mental acumen.

Writing

Many of the activities that keep retirees busy in their golden years are planned based on lifetime dreams, such as dancing, boating, fishing, tennis, golf, and traveling. In Barbara's case, it was her love of dancing that introduced her to writing. She was asked to write a column by the publisher of Long Island's New York Ballroom Dance Newsletter: "Around the Floor." Her column covered our travels around the world and the many dancing experiences we've enjoyed. The newsletter evolved from a local paper into an international website with links around the world, including China, England, Australia, South Africa, Korea, and many Latin American countries. Other links connected to Bridge to World Championships, colleges and universities, Swing dance sites, and, my favorite, Tango dance sites. I soon had a column on the same website under the name, "Tangohombre," covering ballroom dancing on Long Island, with emphasis on the Argentine Tango.

We were fortunate that an opportunity presented itself where Barbara and I could indulge in a pastime that would carry into our retirement years and would keep both of us occupied doing something that we didn't realize we had a passion for until we tried writing. Many of our articles required that we visit various dance clubs on Long Island and report what we experienced. As reporters we were required to interview and mingle with many of the dancers in our dancing network, which opened a whole new world for us as we met and interviewed people that represented every level of ballroom dancing, from world renowned professionals, like Karina Smirnoff, down to beginning students.

The stories that appeared on the website were quite condensed from the original ones submitted to the publisher. At that time, I thought it would be fun to present the articles as they appeared in the newsletter and website, and then tell the full stories as originally experienced by us in a book about dancing. It's quite common that opening one door leads to other doors being opened. In our case, dancing led to writing for a local dance publication and then publishing a book about our travels, with an emphasis on dancing.

In addition to the published articles, many of our dancing experiences were not presented for publication, so I thought, why not include those stories too? It took several years of serious writing on my part, and intense editing by Barbara, to get our 600-plus page book *Dancing Around the World with Mike and Barbara Bivona* published at the beginning of 2010.

Two of the condensed stories, as they appeared in the newsletters, follow:

Traveling Around: "Chicken Soup and Chocolate Pudding," by Barbara Bivona

As a child growing up during World War II in Brooklyn, New York, the popular sound of that era was big band music. We listened to Swing and Jive, ballads alluding to loved ones who were far from home during the war, and patriotic music. The Rumba was making a good showing on the dance floor, and the Andrew Sisters sang "Rum and Coca Cola" to a Rumba beat. I was young and innocent of the ways of the world; my memories of that time were not so much of the devastation and horrors of war, but of growing up in Brownsville, my neighborhood in Brooklyn, my close circle of friends, going fishing with my dad and brother, and my mother's wonderful chicken soup and chocolate pudding. Mom collected records, the old 78 and 33 rpm discs, and was always buying the latest hits. We listened to Helen O'Connell, Buddy Clark, and The Dorsey Brothers; I was amazed when Mom came home with the first LP (long playing) recording that I had ever seen: "Sing, Sing, Sing." Mom would take my hand and dance with me in our tiny living room. If she knew the words, she would sing along with the recording, and my brother George and I would soon join in. That's why, when I saw an ad many, many years later for Joe Battaglia and his New York Band at the Huntington Town House, in Huntington, Long Island, I didn't waste any time making reservations for an evening of dinner and big band dancing.

I was fascinated with Joe's background. Until he retired, he worked in the garment industry in New York City. He started as a young man and after many years of hard work, owned his own business. After retiring, he decided to pursue a life-long dream of taking trumpet lessons. After just six years of lessons, Joe was ready to take on the big band sounds. He played trumpet with several bands and soon decided to form his own, fulfilling another life-long dream. His success was rapid, and soon he and his band were being booked to repeat engagements in New York's theater district and supper clubs. The icing on the cake was a Grammy in the year 2000 for best instrumental recording titled "Close Your Eyes," a tribute to Harry James and Ray Anthony. The band performed music from this album in clubs and is enjoyable either for listening or dancing. That night, we danced to "Embraceable You," "It Had to Be You," "Ain't That a Kick in the Head," as well as more contemporary music, such as "On a Clear Day," and "Misty."

All of these and more are on his album. Joe has been compared to Harry James; however, he told me, "I feel that I have my own sound." And, while he may be using some of Harry James' arrangements, this is definitely not what I would call a cover band. Joe's sounds are his own. True, they are inspired by the master, but they emanate from his own soul. They take me back in time to those wonderful days when my main concerns were homework and what Saturday matinee my friends and I would be seeing at the movie theaters. They take me back to the days of Mom's **Chicken Soup and Chocolate Pudding.**

Barbara occupied many pleasant retirement years visiting different dance venues, locally and globally, and relating her experiences in her "Traveling Around" articles. Of her many stories, I chose to include the one above because it had an exciting retirement story within a story, of Joe Battaglia retiring and fulfilling two of his dreams while in his golden years, which included learning how to play the trumpet and eventually having his own big band. It is living proof that it is never too late to begin exploring new experiences, especially those that stimulate the brain and eventually become a passion and something to look forward to every day during retirement. Joe's story also clearly shows that in many cases, when someone tries something new, it leads beyond the new experience and can open doors to a new lifestyle. Joe's experimenting and passion for playing the trumpet led him to become a big band leader and forever changed his life from being a retired garment industry person to a very active senior citizen. What an incredible change of direction at a time of life when most people are looking to curtail their activities and slow down. His experience certainly describes what baby boomers today describe as "rewiring," instead of retiring. His retirement didn't begin the last chapter of his life but the beginning of a new career that resulted in his record album winning a Grammy Award.

When the publisher of "Around the Floor" asked me to develop a column about Tango dancing and its popularity with today's dancers, I asked him, "Why me?" He said, being that my email address is "Tangohombre" and that Barbara and I studied the Argentine Tango in Buenos Aires, that I probably had some insight into the feel of the Tango and its popularity in today's dance scene. Of course, flattery can go a long way and I decided to give it a try, especially since it would give me an opportunity to visit many dance venues on Long Island, and mingle with people that had a passion for dancing.

As an aside, last night, which was April 5, 2014, we attended a milonga (dance hall) at the GoldCoast Ballroom in Coconut Creek, Florida that featured an exhibition by Gustavo Naveira and partner; he was one of our instructors on our most memorable trip of over 15 years ago to the tango dancing capital of the world, Buenos Aires. It was so exciting to see one of our dance mentors doing a tango dance show. His performance was more than we expected, but what was also more than we expected were the number of people in attendance. The ballroom was filled to capacity, which was lover 400 tango lovers. What was even more surprising were the number of dancers doing the Argentine Tango. There was no room on the large dance floor, boasted to be over 3,000 square feet, to move around comfortably, which resulted in our sitting out many of the dances. Even though the dance floor was crowded, and the milonga began and ended a little late for us, 9 PM to 2 AM, seeing Gustavo dance again was worth the minor discomforts.

One of my first articles as a tango aficionado follows:

Traveling Around: "Tangohombre," by Michael Bivona

When discussing Tango dancing, you might wonder if we are talking about American Tango, International Tango, or the original Argentine Tango. It just so happens that we are referring to all three styles of dancing. Discussing the technical differences on a professional level of these passionate dances is beyond my ability, but I can discuss the differences from my point of view as a social dancer.

About 15 years ago, my wife Barbara and I decided to take dance lessons. We both loved Tango music and decided it would be a good starting dance for us. At the time, the most popular, and probably the only readily available lessons in our area, were in American Tango. The choice of that dance went from a whim to an infatuation and then love in a short time. We became so passionate with the feeling of the dance and the music that we encouraged many of our friends to take Tango lessons.

The image of the actor Anthony Dexter* portraying the great Latin lover Rudolph Valentino in the movie *Valentino* (1951) and dancing a passionate Tango was in my mind often as we progressed with our infatuation with the dance. I recall seeing him portray the great Valentino on screen and remembered how many times my teenage friends and I saw the same picture over and over again, totally absorbed with the music and the passion of the dance.

Over the years, we observed the development of International Tango, enjoying the complexity of the steps, body and head movements, and its strict syllabus. We tried to get into the dance, but for us it lacked the passion and freedom of movement that dancing the other Tangos gave us. Last year, we were invited to participate in an exhibition where the three tangos were performed to show their differences. We danced the Argentine Tango and were followed by a professional-amateur couple dancing the International Tango. The professional, who was from Australia, picked up the mic and said, "Well, you just saw how the Tango came to my country, full of passion and softness of movement, now we will show you how we and the English took the sex out of the dance." Their performance was exemplary, their movements and precision were remarkable; certainly the right dance for competition dancing, but, as social dancers, we still preferred the Argentine Tango. Well, how did we go from the American Tango to the Argentine Tango?

We fell in love with the Argentine style when we saw the show *Tango Argentino* that appeared off-Broadway in Manhattan. Our dance instructor, Electra, of Swing Street Studios in Farmingdale, New York, thought it would be a good idea to expose her students to this type of dancing, so she made a group reservation for the tango dancers in her classes to see the show. That began our journey into the world of Argentine Tango dancing. Little did we know that this style would take many of us to a new level of passion for dancing. We immediately took lessons from Electra, who was waiting for the opportunity to teach this original Tango dance that her father had taught her as a child so many years ago. She had a deep love for the dance, as it brought back memories of when she was a young girl, and of how her parents and their friends, who danced only that style of Tango, would passionately dance till the wee hours of the morning. Thanks to the *Tango Argentino* show, she was able to purchase a great Tango teaching tape and made copies for her students so we could get a true feel for the dance by listening to the sweet, warm, exotic music.

Our lessons were difficult, as we had to learn new patterns that were not familiar to us from other dances that we knew: swaying *cortes (dips)*, body balancing, leg rubs, *ochos* (figure eights), kicks, and the most unusual, stopping to allow your partner to improvise and, in turn, to do the same.

Many years after our introduction to this exotic Tango style, I was reading a travel brochure, *Puente al Tango* (Bridge to the Tango), published by Dan Trenner with a website at www.BridgetotheTango.com. He was organizing a tour to Buenos Aires, Argentina, limited to 40 lucky students. It was an eleven-day tour and included daily lessons, dancing at different *milongas* (clubs) every evening, lectures and demonstrations by the world's great male and female Tango dancers, and most important of all, there was one instructor for every two students. I booked the tour and gave it to Barbara as a birthday gift; luckily, she was as excited as I was about our new adventure.

On our trip, we were taught new *cortes*, turns, kicks, and fine-tuned improvising. But the most exciting and difficult thing to be learned was emphasized by one of our renowned instructors, Mingo Pugliese—**"ATTITUDE."** He said, "There is no dance if you do not have the right **ATTITUDE, not only for the dance, but for life as well."**

That was the end of my article. I wrote about our adventure to Buenos Aires in more detail in my book *Dancing Around the World with Mike and Barbara Bivona.*

*There is an incredible website, "The Anthony Dexter Homepage," established for his memorial, 1913-2001. It includes the theme song for the movie *Valentino*, "Valentino Tango," and the history of this most fascinating and versatile man who played Valentino in the 1951 film. The sophistication of the site is something to behold... **Pure Enjoyment.** Page two of the site is presented below, with the permission of Gilda Tabarez:

View Pictures and Facts about *Valentino* (1951)

Anthony Dexter Photo Gallery
Click on each image to view a larger version.

Memoirs

A nice starting point to keep from getting bored during retirement is to put together the history of your family as far back as you and your relatives can remember. It's certainly helpful if grandparents are living or if they left written histories behind for their heirs to enjoy and explore. While in the process, it's always a good idea to accumulate documentation, when available, for future reference in order to clarify any misunderstanding between friends and relatives—and believe me, there will be lots of discussions and debates about the accuracy of your findings, between family members and sometimes longtime friends.

It's never too early or too late to write a memoir. My friend Murray Soskil wrote his in the twilight years of his retirement. He told me that during WWII, when he was a dogface fighting with the 3rd Division in Europe, he had taken notes of his experiences as a soldier in the United States Army. After the war ended, he put pen to paper and consolidated his notes, ending up with a surprisingly large number of pages outlining his experiences during his time in the military. When he finished, he placed his outline in a box and put it in his attic for future reference. I asked him why he waited until he was almost 90 years old to write his memoir. He said to me, "Get my book *From the Bronx to Berchtesgaden* and you'll have my answer." So, here is his answer, nicely explained in the acknowledgement section of his book that was published in 2012. The excerpts and book cover are presented with the permission of his estate and his wife Pearl:

> I kept a journal during combat and jotted down my experiences when I had time to do so between battles. These notes came in handy after I was discharged and settled at home again, when I decided to write an account of my service in the infantry. Words came to me quickly. Soon, I had finished fifty pages. Then we were occupied with a special event, the birth of my first son. So my story was put on hold and set aside for six decades.

Some years ago, my family was invited to a dedication ceremony in Washington, D.C. for a memorial monument honoring the four hundred thousand servicemen killed during the Second World War. My wife and I, two of my grandsons, and two of my great-grandsons decided to attend.

At the memorial, my grandson typed my name into a computer that was available to those attending the affair, and my picture came up with a list of my citations. Everyone was excited. Many people came over to see what was going on. Several said that to meet a live hero some sixty-odd years later made the day memorable for them.

Eventually, with the urging of my four older grandsons, Mathew, Michael, Eric, and Brett, and my granddaughter, Katelyn, who kept saying, "Poppy, can you tell me some of your war stories," convinced me that I should tell of my experiences. I decided to write this memoir in order to let my children and grandchildren know what it was like being a dogface infantry soldier on the ground in France and Germany during the Second World War.

Unfortunately, while I was busy writing, my friend passed away in 2013, at the age of 91.

A brief biography of Murray as it appears on the WIX website follows:

Murray Soskil was a World War II Veteran from the Bronx, New York. He was the recipient of two silver stars, a bronze star, six battle stars, the French Metal of Valor, the French Foligere, and the Presidential unit citation for service in France and Germany with the 3rd Infantry Division. As a Dogface soldier, he fought from the Colmar Pocket, through the Vosges Mountains, and on to Nuremburg and Munich. Along the way, the 3rd Divisions liberated two concentration camps and captured Hitler's private mountain retreat in Berchtesgaden.

Murray lived at the Polo Club in Boca Raton, Florida with his wife of 70 years, Pearl. They have three sons, ten grandchildren, and ten great grandchildren. In May of 2012, Murray was honored as the *Veteran of the Game* at Citi Field.

A copy of the front cover of his book follows:

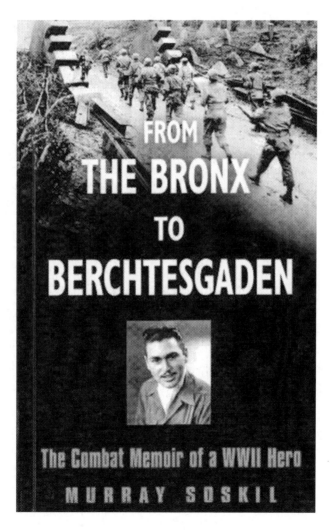

Murray certainly fulfilled his grandchildren's wishes by writing one of the most stunning autobiographies that I have ever read.

One of my most memorable discussions with Murray was when he told me that the Medal of Honor recipient and Hollywood actor Audie Murphy had been in his division. He said: "It's true that he had more medals than me, but to tell you the truth, I was a lot better looking than him." End of story...

Of course, very few people have the heroic past that Murray had, but even so, writing my memoir certainly was an exciting and enlightening chore that I took on when I was in my mid-seventies. My reason for writing my memoir was to permanently record the history of our ancestors that seemed to have become hazy and somewhat confusing over the passing decades. It seemed that many of my relatives had a different story to tell about our family's history. As my parents, grandparents, and their siblings were long departed, I had to do some in-depth research to come up with what we all seemed to agree was an accurate presentation of our ancestry. While I was at it, I thought it would be a good time for me to put in print what the history of my life was. Unfortunately and fortunately, it wasn't as heroic as my friend Murray's, but it detailed my past to the best of my ancient brain's recollection. The result was my book *Was That Me? Turning Points in my Life.*

I began my search by gathering information from my family and friends. Needless to say, there was lots of conflicting information. Between family meetings and numerous emails, we finally decided that the limited information that we had was a good foundation for my writing about our ancestry. My next step was to use the internet to gather additional information that might be useful in my endeavor to trace our ancestors' history. A copy of the cover of my book follows:

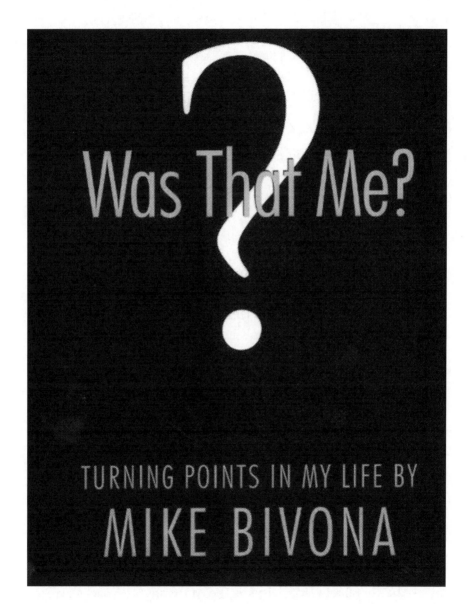

There are literally over a hundred websites that offer assistance in finding ancestry information. Some are free and many charge a fee, depending on the level of service required by the researcher. Some even offer professional help, for a charge, in assisting anyone that prefers having a knowledgeable and unbiased person develop their family tree.

I gathered most of my family's ancestry material from three sources: The Genealogical Research Center at The Library of Congress in Washington, DC; the Mormons' Family History Library in Salt Lake City, Utah, and the Ancestry website (AARP members can get a 30% discount off of the fee on Ancestry's annual membership.)

On one of our annual drives from New York to Florida to escape the North's cold weather, we visited the Library of Congress Complex in the nation's capital and unexpectedly discovered that it had one of the foremost ancestry libraries in the world. We decided to play with one of the many computers that were available to the public to see if we could dig up some family history. After spending a couple of hours tinkering with the keyboard, we became fascinated with some of the information about our families that was stored in their computer's memory bank. From that point on, we were hooked on uncovering information about our ancestry. We also learned that the library had free information on their websites; our favorite was WWW.Archives. gov, which we explored at our convenience whenever time permitted. We were so thrilled that we could gather documented information about our ancestors that we both made notes in our calendars to continue our search ASAP.

Well, a few months went by while we enjoyed ourselves in the Florida sun, swimming, playing golf, and dancing. It seemed as if the search into our pasts sort of ended up on the back burner as we made good use of the Florida weather.

One year, we had booked an American Canyon Tauck Tour before leaving New York; it included Salt Lake City, Utah. Wouldn't you know, the tour included a visit to the Mormon Tabernacle to hear their renowned choir sing. While exploring the religious complex, we learned that they too had an ancestry computerized library equivalent in sophistication to that of the Library of Congress. After enjoying several choir hymns, we headed directly to their library. We were lucky to find two computers that were not in use and renewed our quest for information on our families' backgrounds. What was especially convenient were the Research Consultants and volunteers that were available to help us begin our search. The amazing thing was that their services were free of charge. They were extremely knowledgeable, polite, and attentive. They gave us shortcuts on how to maneuver through their website to retrieve pertinent information efficiently. We spent over an hour at the site, and thanks to their guidance, were able to gather quite a bit of information on the history of some of our ancestors. Unfortunately, we had to rush to catch up with our tour members and continue our journey to the national parks. The Mormons have websites that we used extensively in our research, my favorite was WWW.Myheritage.com.

The third website that we used often was a privately owned one at WWW.Ancestry.com. They offered a two week free trial and various fees based on the length of membership. For instance, there is a monthly charge of $19.95 after the trial or $99.00 for a six month membership. We found that their website and follow-up research was easy to maneuver, so we were paid members until we gathered sufficient information to satisfy ourselves.

I must say that researching our ancestry became a labor of love for me. We even traveled to Italy to visit the Town of Bivona, in the Province of Agrigento, Sicily, from where my father and his parents migrated at the turn of the 20th century. We made the trip with my two sisters, Anne and Mae and Mae's husband Sylvester. Meeting and spending time with the people of the small mountain town that is situated on the top of Mt. Sicani was one of the highlights of our lives.

On one of our other trips to Italy in 1987, we visited my mother's parents' place of birth, San Angelo de Lombardi, which is located in a province outside of Avellino. We were shocked to see that the town had been virtually destroyed by an earthquake in 1980 and was still being reconstructed, but evidently very slowly. Our visit was short, as the noise from the construction throughout the town and the remaining evidence of the earthquake made us decide to continue our journey to a more pleasant place.

Unfortunately, Barbara didn't have the same luck with her research as I did. Her grandparents were from Russia and much of the Russian information pertaining to them was lost during the German invasion of WWII and the many periods of Jewish oppression that was carried out by various heads of state in Russia.

After gathering a considerable amount of historical data about my family, I visited with my living relatives or mailed information to those who were unable to meet with us, and eventually came to a consensus with them about my findings. The result was my book *Was That Me? Turning Points in My Life.* I made sure that all my family members received copies of the book, especially my children and grandchildren, so that they would have a somewhat accurate history of their heritage.

Collecting Books and Reading

Who of us hasn't dreamt of sitting down in a comfortable chair, in a quiet place, without interruption, and reading all the books that we never had a chance to read when we were in our productive time of life with limited time for such a luxury? Well, Barbara and I are among those who just didn't have time between our busy schedules to read all the books we accumulated over the years. We tried during our preretirement years to join book clubs, but could never put the time aside to participate and enjoy the camaraderie and exchange of ideas that is the essence of these clubs. So we did the next best thing; we started collecting books from used book stores in our travels, with the intention that when we had the time in our retirement, we would catch up on all the reading that we missed during our years of employment and raising our family.

Not to say that we didn't get some book reading in, but there were so many books we wanted to delve into, but just couldn't due to the time constraints in our busy lives. Barbara collected as many books as she could get her hands on from her favorite authors, including Stephen King, Dean Koontz, Mary Higgins Clark, Anne Rice, John Saul, and many of the classics. I was always fascinated with information on Christopher Columbus and the Age of Discovery. So I in turn started collecting books from the 14th through the 18th centuries, especially those that pertained to Italian explorers such as Marco Polo, who sailed for Italy and traveled to China overland; Christopher Columbus, who sailed for Spain and added the better part of the "new world" to the holdings of that country; Amerigo Vespucci, who sailed for Spain and supposedly was the first European to realize that the land mass was a new continent; Giovanni da Verrazzano, who sailed for France and explored the East Coast of the new lands, and finally, James Cabot (Giovanni Caboto), who sailed for England and was responsible for adding the northern part of the American continent to the English map of conquests. Captain Caboto had to change his name during his employment with the English Crown as they didn't want the world to think that they had to go outside of their homeland to find someone to head their exploration into the new world.

So, when we retired, we had hundreds of books that we had collected and finally had time to read in the comfort of our home, while sunning ourselves on the beach, and in our travels. It's interesting how one's passion can open doors to other unrelated happenings. Due to my obsession with collecting books and material on Columbus and the Age of Discovery, I became a charter member of the congressionally designated "Christopher Columbus-500 Quincentenaries' Jubilee Commission" and the New York "Countdown 1992" organization that promoted the Expo '92 event. From our association with these organizations, Barbara and I went to Seville, Spain, to take part in the Universal World's Fair-Expo '92, "Columbus and the age of Discovery," as spectators for the New York organization "Countdown 1992." The Expo was from April 29 to October 12, 1992, on La Isla de La Cartuja, in Seville. Over 100 countries were spread out over 500 acres displaying their pride and ethnic joy in every type of exhibition imaginable. We were there for several days, including the finale on October 12, and became part of the history of that event, which recorded over 41 million visitors. A poster of the 1992 Seville-Expo '92 follows:

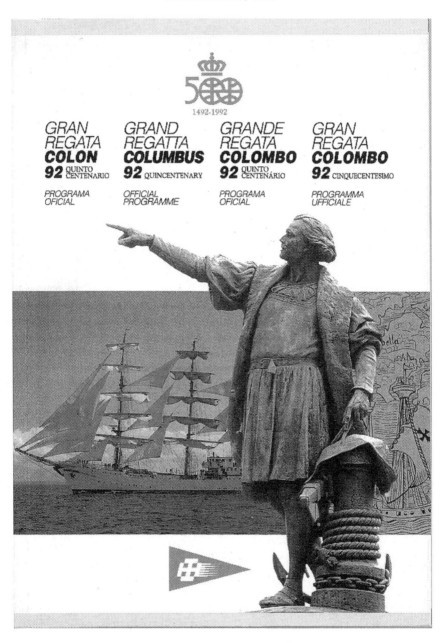

Well into my retirement, I realized that I had collected in excess of 400 books, maps, and documents on the Age of Discovery. I also realized, after a friend's demise, that many of the possessions that he had accumulated over his lifetime and were so dear to him were of no interest to his heirs or friends and were disposed of like pieces of junk. So I began looking for a home for my collection. Providence was instrumental in my having the opportunity to place my collection at the Columbus Foundation, the organization that is the sponsor of the annual Columbus Day Parade in New York City. We were at Dan Maloney's Empress Ballroom in Delray Beach, Florida enjoying our usual Friday night social dance party, when I was introduced to Lou Mangone, who was a member of the foundation and in charge of their library. I mentioned that I was in negotiations with Brown University, in Providence, Rhode Island, about donating some of my collection to their extensive, world-renowned Americana Collection of books on that period.

I was a long-standing member of the Brown University Library and was excited that they were considering adding some of my books to their collection. Lou said his organization would be very interested in my books and could probably keep them as a collection in a separate area of their extensive library as they only had a sprinkling of books about their namesake. The prospect of having the collection stay intact under my name was very compelling; Brown University would have scattered the books in their respective categories throughout their humongous library, which meant that I would lose the recognition of the collection. So, to make a long story short, I indexed my collection and shipped it off to the foundation, where the books reside today for the pleasure of their members and researchers. My fear of having my beloved collection scattered or discarded was no longer a concern; I found a home for it and was very pleased when I visited the foundation and saw a place set aside for my collection. A copy of the foundation's newsletter mentioning my donation follows, as well as a picture of the library that was set aside for the collection:

Michael Bivona Collection:
Columbus, the Age of Discovery and Related Books
Donated, March 2006

Bivona Collection Donated

The Foundation has received an enormously generous and essential donation, the Michael Bivona Collection: Columbus, The Age of Discovery and Related Books. The collection, which Mr. Bivona acquired over the course of 30 years, contains approximately 300 books and immediately gives us an extensive group of works about the Foundation's namesake. It will reside in the Ambassador Charles A. Gargano Library.

"This remarkable donation, by Michael Bivona, vastly increases and improves the quality of our library's holdings," said President Louis Taliarini. " We are deeply grateful to Mr. Bivona for his donation, and we are proud that our Member Louis Mangone made the introduction that has brought the Michael Bivona Collection to the Foundation."

"The age of discovery was roughly 1400 to 1700, and of course Columbus was central to the period," said Mr. Bivona. "He had the audacity and the courage to venture out into unknown areas. At that time, very few people would venture out on the water beyond the sight of land. He had few navigational instruments to guide him when he became the first European to discover and record this unknown continent. He found his way back to Spain using his knowledge of celestial navigation, ocean currents and prevailing winds. The route he took is still being used today because of the favorable winds and currents. What he did was just amazing."

Mr. Bivona, 72, and his wife Barbara live in Dix Hills, Long Island and have two grown children and two grandchildren. Now retired, he was a CPA and co-owner and CFO of Manchester Technologies. His main hobbies are boating and ballroom dancing. He owns a 42-foot Cris-Craft boat, which they've taken to Block Island, Cape Cod, Nantucket and Plymouth, among other places, but, unlike Columbus, he said, "with very sophisticated electronic navigational devices."

Foundation News

Mr. Bivona and Foundation Member Louis Mangone belong to a dancing group that meets regularly. Several months ago, Mr. Bivona was in discussions with Brown University, in Providence, Rhode Island, about donating the collection to the school. "I mentioned to Lou Mangone that I was talking to Brown, and he told me that the Foundation would be interested in the collection." Mr. Mangone pursued the collection, which is now coming to the Foundation.

Book collector, philanthropist and ballroom dance aficionado Michael Bivona with wife Barbara in a tango

The Michael Bivona Collection has great depth in its holdings of books about Columbus, from his own letters and journals and contemporary accounts of his voyages to the works of later historians who interpret and comment on the lasting changes brought about by his explorations. Mr. Bivona acquired the books from every type of source imaginable, from specialized booksellers to bookstores and flea markets, and the books range in age from recent to over 100 years old.

"It is wonderful to know that my collection will have a meaningful place at the Foundation to honor a great explorer," Mr. Bivona said. ❖

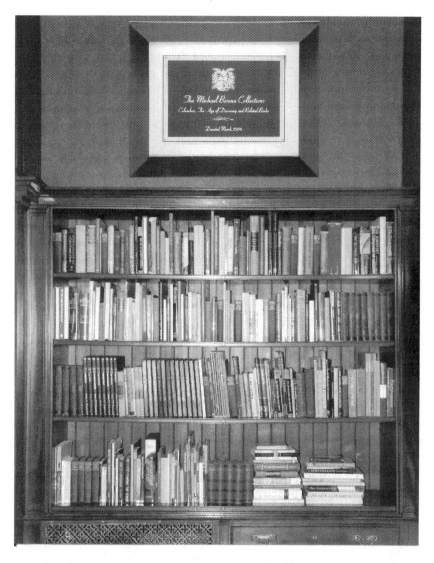

In addition to the wonderful experience of visiting Spain for the 500th anniversary of Columbus's discoveries, earlier in the year we helped New Orleans celebrate the discovery by spending one week on the *Mississippi Queen* Paddlewheel exploring the Mississippi River and a week at Mardi Gras; the theme again was "Columbus and the Age of Discovery." So, my love of reading and my hobby of collecting books of that period resulted in our visiting Spain and New Orleans, chasing our dreams, with two unforgettable lifetime experiences.

I can't express how much pleasure Barbara and I have had over the years collecting and then reading the many books we've accumulated. Collecting and reading books is certainly a pastime that can be enjoyed by everyone, regardless of their financial or physical health. Some books that we purchased cost as little as two dollars. What better way is there to spend some quality time when one's body is aching from advancing age, than by picking up a book, stretching out on a comfortable chair, opening to the first page, and taking part in a new adventure.

Today, the younger generation doesn't seem to enjoy reading from printed pages. Their heads tend to be glued to computer screens of every size. So for those who are not inclined to open a book and explore its contents, there is an alternative that has become very popular with many of the **"electronic folks,"** and that's eBooks. It is an **electronic book** (also known as e-book, eBook or digital book), and seems to be the wave of the future for reading books and magazines. E-books are usually read on dedicated hardware devices known as e-Readers or e-books. The most popular readers are the Amazon Kindle and Barnes & Noble NOOK. For a fraction of the cost of a printed book, the contents can be read using the aforementioned devices for under ten dollars and in many cases at no charge. Many seniors can be seen on air flights to and from Florida enjoying the benefits of the lightweight eBooks; some are so small that they can be put into a pocketbook or inside jacket pocket, which makes it a lot more convenient than carrying a clumsy printed book. Other advantages of the small lightweight devices are the applications that are available for accessing magazines, games, and the Internet. Seniors that do not have eyesight limitations should certainly try using the electronic devices as they are easy to carry around and have an abundance of applications and information that can stimulate a person's brain cells.

For seniors that have eyesight limitations or who would prefer listening to stories, www.audible.com, has thousands of titles available using audiobooks. One of the special benefits of listening to stories with audiobooks is that it brings back memories of when you were a child and your parents read you those wonderful bedtime stories. Many of our annual snowbird car trips were made a lot more comfortable when

Barbara and I listened to stories while driving the tedious roads from New York to Florida, and back again.

Exercising

Wouldn't it have been nice to have started an exercise regimen when we were young and our bodies were flexible and our muscles toned, and to have continued with a healthy routine into our senior years? We certainly know that our bodies were meant to move and the expression "Use it or lose it" certainly applies to body motion and its relationship to exercising. We were taught early on that if our muscles become too flabby and weak that our heart and lungs wouldn't function efficiently, and that our joints would become stiff and easily injured. Not only are our bodies meant to move, they actually crave exercise on a regular basis for physical fitness and good health. According to our doctors, a good exercise and stretching schedule can reduce the risk of heart disease, cancer, high blood pressure, diabetes, and other maladies; plus it will no doubt improve our appearance and delay the aging process.

Knowing all the positive results that can be obtained from a good exercise program, why aren't we more conscientious about keeping active with a regular exercise routine? Well, the obvious reasons are that when we were young, we felt good and probably looked good. We were busy working and raising a family, and doing any activity on a regular basis that required time and energy wasn't easy. The one thing that most of us didn't have in our younger lives was spare time, which unfortunately put exercising on the bottom of the list of "things to do that I like." Most of us begin an exercise program out of necessity rather than on a voluntary basis; at least that's the way Barbara and I began our journey into a healthier lifestyle that continues well into our senior years.

In 1988, when Barbara was 52 years of age, we drove our oldest child Stephen to the State University at Albany, NY to begin his life as a college student. After helping him move into the 17-story dormitory, which took a better part of the day, we checked into the Ramada Inn in town and had a leisurely dinner and a well-deserved night's sleep.

In the morning, we decided that Barbara would take the first leg of our 200-mile trip back to Long Island, and that I would finish driving the last part of the journey. Well, as "the best laid plans of mice and men" don't always go according to plans, that day was the beginning of a horrific nightmare. A few minutes after awakening and discussing our plans for the day, Barbara had a seizure and passed out. I couldn't revive her and quickly called the hotel manager, who appeared as soon as I hung up the phone. He called for an ambulance and within minutes Barbara was on her way to the Albany Medical Center, which, thank God, was a short five-minute ride from the hotel. After a CAT scan, it was determined that she had an aneurysm that had burst in the left side of her head and the prognosis was not very good. I was told to make funeral arrangements, as the chances of her surviving the night were very slim.

Needless to say, I was in a state of shock; she was very rarely sick during our 20-plus years of marriage, and being told that we were going to lose her seemed to be an impossibility that my mind would not accept. I wasn't too sure about the quality of the hospital, so I called my doctor back home and inquired about the credentials of the facility. I was told by him and others that I called that the Albany Medical Center was one of the best facilities in the country for taking care of the serious medical problem that she had.

I was also told by my regular doctor to make sure that the Chief of Staff of Neurosurgery was assigned to her case. I insisted that Doctor Pop handle her, which he did to perfection. He told me that he would have to wait until her brain settled from the blood burst, and when she was strong enough, he would perform an operation and remove the blood from her agitated brain and hopefully insert a metal clip on the weak part of the vessel that had caused the aneurysm. It took a week before she had enough strength for him to perform the critical operation, and two additional weeks for her to recover. After three weeks at the center, we were able to take her home for her long three-month recovery. During my three-week stay in Albany, my 18-year-old son had to plough his way through the beginning of his first semester at the university, and my 16-year-old daughter Laurie, who was starting a new term in high school, had to fend for herself back on

Long Island. Fortunately, my brother Vic and sisters Anne and Mae and their spouses Rose and Sal made sure that someone was with me every day during that trying time. The only bright side to the experience was that Barbara didn't have the seizure while driving the first part of our trip back to our home or we both would probably have perished in a car crash, taking God only knows how many other people with us.

Well, what does all this have to do with exercising? As any good doctor will tell someone that is recuperating from surgery, exercising is paramount to recovery and a healthy life. Barbara followed the good doctor's advice and began a walking regimen that eventually included some of the girls in our neighborhood. She and her friends walked for three days a week, and in inclement weather, they would happily walk through the local mall, rewarding themselves with serious shopping when their routine was done. So there we have it: out of necessity due to an horrific experience, my wife began her exercise program that would last into retirement. But, her experience didn't encourage me to start an exercise program, as I felt great and looked pretty good in my friendly mirror. It took a big "Kick in the ass" for me to wake up and begin my exercise routine.

In 1993, when I was 59, I went for a stress test and failed dismally. My story began when my good friend and fellow worker, Charles Kaufman, age 42, had a heart attack and died on the spot. He was the youngest of the executives in our company and the shock of his passing made the remaining 12 officers think hard about their sedentary lives. We decided that we should all have thorough medical exams, including stress tests, to see if we were possibly candidates for joining Chuck in the hereafter. Well, to make a long story short, everyone passed with flying colors, except for me. I was taken off the treadmill before the test was over and told to rest; it seemed my heart was jumping all over the place. Although I was the oldest in the group, I thought that my body was in better shape than most, as I was only slightly overweight and stayed pretty active with boating and dancing whenever I had the time. The only discomfort I experienced at that time was occasional heartburn. The cardiologist told me that I had to undergo an angiogram to determine which arteries were clogged. He also told me not to drive or go to work until the test was done. I immediately went into denial and walked out of his office in a state of confusion; my wife, who was waiting for me, seemed to be in an even greater state of confusion when I told her of my unhappy experience. A couple of days later, I went to St. John's Hospital in Smithtown and had the procedure done. While under valium—thank God for the pacifying drug—I was told that a heart attack was imminent and that I should be transported immediately to St. Luke's Hospital in Manhattan for open heart surgery. As I was still in a happy mood from the drug, I agreed and within a short period of time I was strapped onto a gurney, with an intravenous shunt in my arm, and was on my way by ambulance from Smithtown to New York City, which took over two very long hours.

It was determined that I needed double bypass open heart surgery. My two main arteries were 90 and 70 percent closed and had to be bypassed using both mammary arteries from my chest, which were supposed to be the preferred arteries to use in that type of procedure. Still under the influence of the peaceful drug, I agreed to everything the doctors said, and the next day the operation was done successfully, although I didn't remember a thing and awoke two days later with all the usual tubes sticking into my body and my brother Vic leaning over my bed.

His first words that I remember so clearly were, "Are you sure you needed this operation?" That was his sense of humor and it caused me to laugh and disrupt some of the tubes that made me look like a Borg from the series *Star Trek*. Because of some blood complications, I spent 11 days in the hospital instead of the usual week, and when I finally got home and looked in the mirror, I didn't recognize the emaciated person starring back at me. In that short period of time, my muscles had atrophied and I looked ten years older.

In a little over a month, I was driving my car and was able to return to work. The doctors insisted that I begin a physical therapy program, preferably at the St. John's Hospital gym. I agreed, knowing that if I was left unsupervised, that in time I would lose interest in working out and would return to my old bad habits that were probably responsible for my medical emergency. The program consisted of working out at their gym for two days a week for one hour each day with other recuperating heart patients. I continued for almost two years, using treadmills, bicycles, Stairmasters, and minor weights. The therapy began slowly and in time my muscles and speed surpassed my levels prior to the surgery. When exercising became a permanent part of my lifestyle, I began working out at Bally's gym and eventually bought equipment that I was accustomed to for my finished basement. It took a medical emergency for me to start living a healthier life, which included exercising, the Mediterranean diet, and stress avoidance, when possible. One of the things that kept me on a strict low fat diet was that my wife Barbara, who is still quite slim, went on the same diet that my doctors insisted I go on.

One of the most bewildering things about retiring is that there doesn't seem to be enough time to do the things that are planned; we always seem to be running out of time and in a rush to get things done. So, out of desperation, I developed a **priority list** to remove the stress that accompanies the feeling of not getting things accomplished in a timely manner. The list follows:

1-Excercising three times a week.
2-Dancing, at least twice a week.
3-Writing as much as possible (I'm now on my sixth book).
4-Boating and fishing, whenever the opportunity arises.
5-Golf in good weather only.
6-Charitable work, whenever the need arises.

If there is ever a conflict in any of the above, I always try to use my **priority list** as a guide; for instance, if there is a dance on a particular night and a golf game scheduled for the same day, the golf game is skipped as it is number 5 and dancing number 2 on my list.

One of the advantages of an exercise schedule during retirement, if planned properly, is that we have all the time necessary to firm up. We always seemed to have had excuses, when we were in our productive working years and raising families, for not having enough time to take care of our bodies through proper exercise. In the golden years of our lives, what better way is there than spending a few hours a week at a gym or in our homes using equipment of our choice? Many people use the excuse that they play baseball, golf, tennis, or many of the other physical sports, so they don't have to enter an exercise program. I found that to enjoy the full potential of any sport, one must be in good physical condition, and it's not the sport that gets you there, it's the condition that is developed by working out on a regular basis that makes you excel at any sport. In our case, we certainly couldn't do ballroom dancing at an aerobic level if we weren't in good physical condition. Therefore, my advice to retired folks is to stretch for at least 15 minutes every morning before getting out of bed, and exercise three times a week from 45 minutes to one hour. For those not inclined to working out indoors, aggressive outdoor walking, cycling, or swimming are good alternatives, but should be done consistently and scheduled for at least three days a week. As previously mentioned, ballroom dancing done in earnest is certainly an aerobic activity and so are many of the popular line exercises such as Zumba and Dancercise, which are done to music and are favorites with the ladies. None of these activities should be tried unless the participants are in relatively good physical shape before the activity, and at the beginning should be supervised by a professional, as unconditioned bodies can be damaged if not properly prepared for the task. Always remember, before participating in any physical activity, stretch for at least 10 to 15 minutes; it prepares your muscles for the forthcoming strenuous events. And above all, make sure that you discuss any new activities that you might consider with your doctor, as he might suggest the types of activities that are best for your present physical condition.

Traveling

Traveling is without a doubt on the top of a retiree's **"list of things to do** before I **kick the bucket."** I thought I would write about two of the many trips we took that might be of interest to my readers. Everyone dreams of going to New Orleans Mardi Gras, so that will be the first adventure that I will write about. Second, I will write about our many trips to the capital of the United States, Washington, DC, and our experiences at many of the Smithsonian Institute's museums and parks, where many opportunities exist for retirees to toy with the idea of working part-time or as volunteers at many of their venues.

New Orleans Mardi Gras

Our journey began when I opened my daily mail and a colorful brochure stood out from the other documents; it was a vacation invitation from the Delta Steamboat Company requesting our presence on one of their Mississippi River cruises. The one that caught my eye was a theme cruise featuring Big Bands, such as Guy Lombardo's Royal Canadians and Les Elgart and his Manhattan Swing Orchestra. The cruise coincided with the annual New Orleans Mardi Gras and the "500th Centennial of the Discovery of America" by the Italian explorer Christopher Columbus, which was the main theme of the festival. Well, there it was: Barbara's childhood dream of traveling down the Mississippi River with Tom Sawyer and Huck Finn on a paddlewheel boat, and my dream of going to the Mardi Gras festival in New Orleans. Both of our dreams of sailing on a Showboat (like the one in the great musical of that name) with Big Band music, and my passion and infatuation with collecting books on the Age of Discovery, especially concerning the great navigator, Christopher Columbus, were all in one package, with Mardi Gras thrown in as a bonus.

Barbara and I couldn't believe that so many of the items on our *Bucket List* could be realized on one vacation. We figured that we could take a riverboat trip on the *Mississippi Queen* Paddlewheel for seven days, which began and ended in New Orleans, and then extend our trip to include six days in a centrally located hotel around Bourbon Street, so we could really get into the Mardi Gras spirit. We had spent a previous vacation in New Orleans many years before, but not at festival time—although it does seem that every day in New Orleans is a festival. We were familiar with the layout of the area and what would be the most advantageous location for our stay. On our prior visit to the city, we had stayed at the Royal Sonesta Hotel in the Bourbon Street area, but the people and traffic noise made the stay less desirable then we hoped for. We did have occasion to enjoy a great dinner in an upscale restaurant at the 17-floor Hotel Monteleone in the French Quarter off of Bourbon Street, which was located in a less noisy location than the other hotel, especially in the rooms on the upper floors. It also boasted a rooftop swimming pool with spectacular views of the French Quarter and the historic city. With this information in mind, we called our travel agent, Barbara, at Liberty Travel and told her what our plans were and asked her to put together a travel package for us. Considering that the trip would be quite extensive and somewhat complicated, we decided to leave all the arrangements and details in her experienced hands. Our decision turned out to be a wise one; within a week, she laid out our itinerary, including all the sightseeing that we planned plus some extra goodies, like attending a Grand Mardi Gras Ball.

We flew American Airlines to New Orleans, and that's when the fun began. Our luggage didn't appear on the arrival carousel; the sinking feeling in my stomach got worse when we were the only passengers left waiting for our baggage to appear. After wasting a couple of hours with representatives of the Steamship Company and American Airlines, and filling out numerous forms describing our missing property, we left the airport and took a taxicab to the New Orleans Port where our ship was docked. The cab driver got lost in a downpour of rain that restricted his visibility. I brought to his attention that what seemed to be the buildings of the city were behind us; he said, "Sorry, my mistake" and then turned his cab around in the right direction. We finally got to the embarkation port just as the rain stopped. There was a small crowd of people on the dock in a covered area enjoying the music provided by a small combo band, while imbibing drinks provided by several waitresses from the ship. I immediately had a scotch and water, which was my drink of choice in those days, and before I knew it, down went several more, but to no avail. I was so hyper from the loss of our luggage and the possibility of going on a two-week vacation with little or no clothes, which was exacerbated by our getting lost on the way to the ship, that I was convinced that the whole journey was going to turn out to be a disaster. Barbara, although upset, tried to calm me down. She wasn't overly concerned, as the prospect of buying a new wardrobe for the trip didn't seem to be an unhappy event for her. My mind formed prayers, hoping that the representative of the steamship company, who remained behind at the airline terminal, would locate our baggage. Until then, we just had to make the best of a combination of unfortunate events.

We boarded the paddlewheel and checked with the ship's coordinator, who informed us that due to our misfortune, they were upgrading our room at no charge, to a full suite. Well, maybe things were starting to turn around; in time, my drinks did their job, and I calmed down quite a bit, returning to my optimistic, fun-loving self.

We went to dinner and felt the boat moving away from the dock, which brought back the helpless feeling that one gets when unpleasant things happen that are out of their control; where was our luggage and what could happen next? How would we replace all of our personal belongings? The delicious French cuisine that evening tempered my feeling of anxiety, somewhat, but sharing a bottle of wine with Barbara was more effective. We hurried back to our cabin, opened the door, and miracles of all miracles, our baggage was staring at us. I lifted a piece, and panic returned; the luggage was weightless. Now we had our bags, but there was nothing in them. Unbeknownst to us, our cabin steward had unpacked our bags and put our belongings in the dressers and closet. We both collapsed on the queen-size bed and just remained silent and motionless for about 15 minutes. We regained our composure, freshened up, and journeyed to the lounge area for orientation and to meet our fellow passengers.

When retiring for the evening, we both agreed that we should put the day behind us and erase the mishaps from our minds. Hopefully, we would continue with our wonderful vacation with no further unhappy incidences. Mark Twain aptly said, "The face of the river, in time, becomes a wonderful book...not one to be read once and thrown aside, for it has a new story to tell every day." Well, we were hoping for a new story when we woke up the following morning.

And a new story it was. The sun peeked through our partially opened drapes; fresh Mississippi River air forced its way into our senses, while a whiff of bacon and eggs floating by got our attention, so we quickly dressed and hastened to the place creating the aroma. I would have been content to just sit on one of the outside chaise lounges and breathe in the fresh air and intoxicating aroma from the food being prepared for our morning meal. What a wonderful beginning to a new day. After breakfast, the first mate took some of us on a guided tour of the *Mississippi Queen*. His dissertation was robotic, but precise as to the history and specifications of the paddlewheel. He said:

> The boat was built in 1976 in celebration of the bicentennial and, when built, was the largest steamboat in existence. It is 382 feet long, 68 feet wide, weighing 3,364 tons, has 208 staterooms accommodating 422 passengers with a complement of over 100 crew members and staff. The red circular paddlewheel itself weighs 70 tons; located forward of it, at the stern of the boat, is the largest steam driven calliope on the river, boasting 44 pipes, whose music is magical and can be heard for five miles, when announcing the majestic ship's presence on the river. The décor of the boat is Americana, with floral wallpaper and matching fabric, beveled mirrors, crystal chandeliers, and polished brass railings. The staircases are red carpeted with ornate wooden hand rails; chairs and accessories are in the Victorian style. The Grand Saloon is the center of activity and is used as a showroom and gathering place; its dance floor is large enough to accommodate the swinging dancers on the ship.

My favorite place, the wheelhouse, was forward; what a thrill it was to steer the ship—with the captain's permission of course, and under his watchful eyes. He let me navigate an easy part of the river for about five minutes. "The steamboats were finer than anything on shore—like palaces." Mark Twain was right when he wrote those words in his book *Life on the Mississippi*. I was navigating a palace down the waterway, with images of the great river flowing through my mind from the Broadway musical *Showboat*. I was humming the river's song, "Old Man River," and, for a few minutes, I became a riverboat captain transporting my passengers and cargo to the far-away towns along the majestic river during the heyday of the paddlewheel boats.

We spent a relaxing and friendly day traveling on the majestic river, making friends, and just enjoying the homey feeling that is so prevalent on small river boats. A big difference compared to cruising on a large ocean liner is that the staff of the river boats were all American, not what we experienced when traveling on larger vessels, where most of the crew members and staff were usually foreigners with difficult names to remember. It didn't take us long to get used to the odiferous surroundings in the air of deep Southern fried cooking and the comforting feeling of the sun resting on my body as I enjoyed reading some of Mark Twain's adventures, while spread out on a chaise lounge, in the open air at the stern of the boat, lulled by the rhythm of the bright red paddlewheel and dozing into dreamland between paragraphs.

The ship's small combo band of six, including two pianists, played music on and off all day. Their sounds floating through the air, mixing with the heavenly aroma of our next meal, gave me the feeling of being at a carnival. Dinner was a cholesterol nightmare; Barbara and I ordered the same food: Southern fried chicken, tons of biscuits, candied beans, and, for dessert, Shoo Fly Pie. It took many turns around the boat to try to alleviate the guilt of overeating before we came to terms with the fact that we were on vacation and an occasional "pig out" wasn't going to kill us, at least not right away.

After dinner, we followed the sound of music to the Grand Saloon, where Les Elgart's Manhattan Swing Orchestra had guests busy on the dance floor doing a Cha-Cha. It was surprising how many single ladies were in attendance, but the cruise operators evidently anticipated this and provided male hosts to dance and talk with the girls throughout the evening. Between sessions, the ship's smaller band entertained us with light jazz and singing from their female vocalists. We danced until the wee hours and returned to our upgraded suite, content that the forgettable mishaps we experienced were being replaced by "happy times." We decided to save our complimentary bottle of champagne, that was nicely presented in our cabin, for another time, but the temptation of the chocolates resting on our bed was too much to resist, so we munched while listening to the smooth-lazy-soft-piped-in-music, and concluded a relaxing, pleasant day on the Mississippi River, as we entered from the beginning of a dream vacation into our evening's dreamland.

We were awakened the next morning by the ship's deafening steam whistle, toot-toot-toot, which announced to the town of Natchez, and everyone else within listening range, that we were coming to town to explore its beauty and meet the local folks. One of the ship's pianists joined in on the calliope and began harmonizing with the whistle's tooting. We again followed the scent of bacon and eggs and, after indulging in a hearty, buy not so healthy breakfast; we disembarked and stepped onto the hospitable soil of Natchez. A committee of the townspeople and a small brass band greeted us to their historic antebellum town. We planned on spending time exploring the town and visiting at least one of the plantations that were located in and around the quaint settlement.

The area of the town that we were in dates back to the 8th century, when the Natchez Indians were masters of that part of the country. Built on the site of an ancient Indian village, it takes its name from that tribe. Around 1730, after several wars, the French defeated the inhabitants and dispersed the Native Americans, keeping many as slaves. Today, most of the remaining Natchez tribe has integrated with the Chickasaw, Creek, and Cherokee Indians, and are mainly in Oklahoma within the Cherokee and Creek nations, quite a distance from their ancestral lands. The town boasts a population of about 18,000 people, including some Natchez Indians, who are the descendants of French slaves. It is probably one of the oldest cities in North America; it is elegant, well preserved, and a showcase for antebellum homes and magnificent plantations. Walking through the town was a throwback to pre-Civil War times, especially when viewing locations where townsfolk were dressed in period costumes, I'm sure for the benefit of tourists such as myself, who were totally captivated by the charade.

Like many Southern towns, the fragrance of flowers, particularly magnolias, freely occupied the air to the enjoyment of its recipients. We couldn't avoid walking into the Stanton Hall Plantation, which occupies a full block in the town. It was built between 1851–1857 for Frederick Stanton, a cotton broker, who went to great lengths to import building materials from Europe, such as moldings, marble fireplace mantles, wrought ironworks, and a great deal of the furnishings, some of which are still intact and displayed throughout the mansion. The entrance immediately impresses visitors with its 17-foot-high ceiling and 72-foot-long hallway. The parlor displayed gilded French mirrors and the fireplaces and mantles throughout were stunning in color and glaze. While exploring the mansion, the smell of buttered biscuits caught our attention; we were pleased to learn that the mansion, which became a National Historic Landmark in 1974, had its own restaurant, The Carriage House. The stately gardens were inviting and spending a few minutes enjoying the colorful flowers and topiary, while sitting on a bench, was refreshing and tranquil.

The compelling "call of the biscuits" coming from the Carriage House finally overcame us and we went with haste to the place where the hypnotic aroma was being created. We had our favorite foods: biscuits with gravy, fried chicken legs, toasty fries, berry ice tea, and more biscuits. The steamboat's whistle, toot-toot-toot, announced that it was time for us to return. The following is a picture of the beautiful lady:

When we returned to our cabin, neatly placed on our bunk were written instructions and competition rules for the dance contest that was to be held that evening. There was also fabric laid out for us to make costumes for the Mardi Gras party, which was to be held on the last day of our cruise, while heading back for the live New Orleans festival. Much to do and so little time to do it in! We were novice dancers at that time and were embarrassed to enter a dance contest, especially having seen some pretty good dancers on the floor the night before. The competition rules were trophies for first, second, and third place in Cha-Cha, Rumba, Foxtrot, Waltz, and Swing, and a special trophy for best overall dancers. No professionals, dance hosts, or crew members were allowed to enter the contest. We only knew the basics to all the dances except for Swing, which we had taken some lessons in over the past year. So we reluctantly entered the Swing contest, just to get into the spirit of things.

The music from Les Elgart's Band could be heard throughout the boat. We followed his sound to the Grand Saloon, where many of the passengers were warming up their dance routines in preparation of the competition. We were both intimidated by the better dancers showing their skills on the dance floor and were inclined to withdraw from the event, but we gathered our courage and picked up our numbers 25 and pinned them onto each other's clothing. It didn't take long for us to realize that we made the right decision in entering the competition, which resulted in our meeting new friends at a very rapid pace. Before the main event, everyone on the dance floor had a great time moving and jumping around to the sound of the band, while changing partners, on cue, from the boat's dance master, which also enhanced our becoming friendly with many of the passengers. The various dance competitions had from 15 to 20 couples in each category ranging from beginners to somewhat good dancers, but absolutely no top-notch dancers, which made the atmosphere a lot less tense for us. The judges included some dance hosts and different ranks of crew members; all in all, they did a commendable job in judging the contestants. It seemed that everyone won a prize, including us for coming in third place in Swing dancing. The evening felt more like a jamboree than a dance competition, and the atmosphere was relaxed and jovial without the stress that usually accompanies dance competitions. We ended the evening as champions, as did everyone else, and retired to our cabin after wishing our many new friends a "fond farewell until the morrow."

We were again awakened by the toot-toot-toot of the steam whistle, reminding us that today we had a race with the Mississippi Queen's older sister, *Delta Queen*, which was the undisputed current paddlewheel champion on the river. According to our ships historian:

> The Delta Queen was born in 1927, weighed 1,650 tons, is 285 feet long and 60 feet wide, and carries 200 passengers and 80 crew members. She is quite a small ship compared to her younger sister, which is 3,364 tons, 383 feet in length, 68 feet in width, and carries 422 passengers with over 100 crew members. But, the Delta is a feisty ship and has won the symbolic "Golden Antlers," which she proudly displayed below her pilot house attesting to the fact that she is the fastest steamboat on the Mississippi River (based on her pilot's expertise and having won their last annual encounter). The history of the Golden Antlers dates back to 1963 when the steamships, *Belle of Louisville* and the *Cincinnati Delta Queen*, ran their first race. It was a 14-mile battle up and down the Ohio River on the first Wednesday in May before the Kentucky Derby. Over the years, the race has been drawing as much attention from the locals as the Derby race. Since then, the boats race against each other every year prior to the Kentucky Derby, for the bragging rights of "the fastest boat on the river," and for the coveted Golden Antlers. The antlers are from an elk and are sprayed gold, signifying the sleekness and speed of the animal and the purity of gold. Our race with the champion will begin at "Dead Man's Bend" and will end at "Washout Bayou." These names conjured up all kinds of images; various stories have come down through the years and have been repeated so often that they are accepted as fact. One of the more popular myths is that over 150-years ago, during the heyday of the rootin' tootin' steamboat era, the river landings were lawless and violent places to live. The most popular of

these roughhouse places was the Natchez-Under-the-Hill Landing, located just below the bluffs overlooking the river at Natchez, Mississippi. There were brawls and knife fights daily; so violent was the neighborhood that the local police would not venture down Silver Street, which stretched from the top of the bluffs down to the river's edge. It was a busy stop for steamboats and a hangout for cutthroats, thieves, mustached gamblers, and ladies of the night. With all that violence, there were always dead bodies that had to be disposed of, and the river was a convenient repository. The bodies would float down to the bend in the river and accumulate there. Many of the corpses that were retrieved still had knives protruding from their decaying bodies, hence the name "Dead Man's Bend."

The crew members spent the morning decorating our boat with banners, and placed noise makers throughout the vessel for our use to add some sound to the festivities. The male crew members dressed in period costumes; many were mustached gamblers, gentlemen of the day, or other unsavory-looking characters. The girls wore riverboat attire from that era, which included frills on their beautifully colored dresses, fancy hats, and pom-poms for the cheerleaders. The calliope played continuous music, including some songs of Stephen Foster, such as "Oh' Susanna," "Nelly was a Lady," "Nelly Bly," "Old Folks at Home," "My Old Kentucky Home," and of course, "De Camp Town Races."

The *Delta Queen* pulled alongside us and blew her challenging whistle loud and clear, "toot-toot-toot." Our response was a spontaneous, "toot-toot-toot." Back and forth they went with the whistle blowing and music playing from their respective calliopes, battling each other for the supremacy of the air and waterway. In addition to the *Delta's* jazz band playing on her bow, the passengers on board seemed to be having a post-victory celebration—a little prematurely for our taste, so we also started singing, howling, and making all sorts of loud sounds with our noisemakers trying to drown out the boisterous celebration of their anticipated victory.

A whistle blast from the *Delta* signaled the start of the race; being the smaller and lighter of the two vessels, she was off and running ahead of us with ease. We struggled for what seemed to be an eternity to get our heavier craft ahead, but to no avail; even though our boat had more powerful engines, we had trouble keeping up with the little lady. The little mistress moved ahead; its pilot evidently had more experience than ours, and found more of the slow water (slack water), which allows a boat to move with less resistance and, therefore, more speed. Near the end of the race, our boat's engines began to show their strength and started pulling up to her older sister; inch by inch we finally caught up, but it was too late. The *Delta* seemed to become jet propelled as we approached and crossed the finish line ahead of us by several boat lengths. She would retain her title as queen of the Mississippi and hold on to her "Golden Antlers" until challenged again by a faster boat. The celebration noise became louder from her majesty as she sped away, whistle blowing and calliope singing, while the passengers swayed to the jazz band's rhythmic sounds, waving goodbye to our losing vessel. Her bright red paddlewheel churned and splashed water far and high as the boat picked up steam and disappeared around the bend and out of sight.

We were greeted by brass bands and the local citizenry when we visited Vicksburg, Mississippi and Baton Rouge, Louisiana. Although we enjoyed the food and history of both places, our minds were on our last stop, New Orleans. During the week, Guy Lombardo's Royal Canadians replaced Les Elgart's band. We couldn't be more excited as he was a Long Island, New York resident and while alive, conducted the world-renowned New Year's Eve orchestra that played at the dropping of the ball in New York City at midnight. In preparation of our visiting the "City of Sin," we prepared our costumes for the Mardi Gras Ball that we were having on the last day of our voyage. Barbara created an outfit that looked like a large salmon: pinkish sequins, with drawings that resembled fish scales. The strange thing about it was her head sticking out from the fish's mouth and her little feet protruding from the fish's tail, but overall her walking fish was quite effective. I took the easy road and made a toga from a white sheet and wore a Roman laurel wreath painted gold on my head, which I put together with some of the material supplied by the crew.

The ball was visually bizarre; there was a variety of fish, many men and women dressed in togas (but not as good as mine), mustached gamblers all over the place, and lots of girls dressed as ladies-of-the-night. We danced and sang the night away to the sweet music of Guy Lombardo's band, which wasn't an easy task, especially if your costume was bulky like Barbara's. Her fish's stomach kept getting in the way of our dancing close, and my toga had the habit of sliding off my shoulder showing my hairy chest. But, all in all, the evening was delightful, especially the laughs at seeing such strange creatures jumping around trying to dance without tripping on themselves or their partners. We raised our champagne glasses to the music of Guy Lombardo's Royal Canadians, and ended the evening singing "Auld Lang Syne." To help us with the words we were given an envelope marked "Don't Open till Midnight." An English version was written in large clear letters, so we could all enjoy singing the whole song. The words were somewhat bastardized from a poem written by Robert Burns in 1788. Here is the rendition that we sang:

> Should old acquaintance be forgot, and never brought to mind?
> Should old acquaintance be forgot, and auld lang syne?
> For auld lang syne, my dear, for auld lang syne.
> We'll take a cup of kindness yet, for auld lang syne.
> And surely you'll buy your pint cup! And I'll buy mine!
> And we'll take a cup of kindness yet, for auld lang syne.
> We two have run about the slopes, and picked the daisies find.
> But we've wandered many a weary foot, since auld lang syne.
> We two have paddled in the stream, from morning sun till dine.
> But seas between us broad have roared since auld lang syne.
> And there's a hand my trusty friend! And give us a hand of thine!
> And we'll take a right good-will draught, for auld lang syne.
> We'll take a cup of kindness yet, for auld lang syne.

We woke up the next morning in New Orleans and spent a week celebrating Mardi Gras with other exuberant revelers. The experience was what we expected; from the time we disembarked to the time we boarded our plane to return home, we made merry, merry, merry, every hour of every day...

For those readers who might be interested in a more detailed story of our *Mississippi Queen* voyage and our week at New Orleans' Mardi Gras, my book *Traveling Around the World with Mike & Barbara Bivona—Part One* can be read as an eBook or a printed book.

Washington, D.C.

Our visits to the nation's capital became an annual event for us on our drive from New York to Florida, and occasionally on our return trips. What attracted us to the District of Columbia were the many museums and other places of interest that seem to be located in every corner of the area. The reason that it's an advantageous place for seniors is that visiting the various locations requires time, and the one thing that we are constantly looking for are places to occupy our time and hopefully enrich our lives. So what better place to spend some quality time than in the capital of our country, where there are no entrances fees at any of the museums? A bonus is to visit in the springtime when colorful cherry blossoms change the concrete background of the buildings into a picturesque pink painting. One of the best reasons for our stop in the capital is it gives us an opportunity to visit with my son, his wife and my two grandchildren, Ian and Katie, who live a short distance away in the town of Burke, Virginia. In addition to our visits becoming a family tradition, it also gives us the opportunity to visits the capital's Smithsonian Museums of our choice free of any charges.

A little history about the Smithsonian Institution, taken from their archives, will shed some light on the complexity and uniqueness of the organization:

> It was funded from a fluke bequest to the United States by the British scientist James Smithson (1764–1829), who had never visited our new democracy. In his will, he stipulated that should his nephew die without heirs,

the Smithson estate would go to the government of the United States to create an "Establishment for the increase and diffusion of Knowledge among men." After his nephew died without heirs in 1835, President Andrew Jackson informed Congress of the bequest, which amounted to a little over $500,000 (about $11,000,000 in current value). The money was invested in shaky state bonds, which quickly defaulted. After years of heated debates in Congress (so what's new?), the Massachusetts Representative (and former President) John Quincy Adams successfully argued that the lost funds plus interest should be restored and used for its original purpose. Congress finally accepted the legacy as intended and pledged the faith and support of the United States to the charitable trust.

In the meantime, the United States Exploring Expedition of the U.S. Navy circumnavigated the globe between 1838 and 1842 and returned with thousands of animal specimens, 50,000_various plants, diverse shells and minerals, tropical birds, jars of seawater, and ethnographic artifacts from the South Pacific. In addition, several military and civilian surveys of the American West, including the Mexican Boundary Survey and Pacific Railroad Surveys, assembled many Native American artifacts and natural history specimens, which they brought to the Capital. So within the first 50 years of our independence, the new democracy was on its way to developing what would become the largest museum complex in the world. The big question was what to do with all that stuff? Our government and private donors decided to begin a building program in the capital to house the collections that were pouring in from the new nation's expansion programs, resulting in the institution currently employing over 6,000 federal employees, and in its latest budget request, after considering the income from the original endowment, contributions, and profits from its retail operations, the federal government was asked to contribute an additional $800 million to allow the institution to continue to pay for the salaries, excellent upkeep of over 136 million items in its collections at 19 museums, its zoo, and its nine research facilities. The facilities are located in Washington, DC, New York City, Virginia, and Panama, and are associated with 168 other affiliate museums from around the world. It also publishes the monthly *Smithsonian* and bimonthly *Air & Space* magazines; quite an accomplishment in less than 200 years.

The National Zoological Park, also referred to as the National Zoo, is part of the Smithsonian complex, which is located in the Capital, and is also worth a visit by seniors, and will be especially exciting and memorable if children and grandchildren can share the experience, as we were fortunate enough to do. A great treat is the "Snore and Roar" event that is sponsored by the "Friends of the National Zoo" (FONZ), a non-profit membership organization. The event allows individuals and families to spend a night at the zoo, in sleeping bags inside of tents. A late-night flashlight tour of the zoo and a two-hour exploration of an animal house or exhibit area are led by a zookeeper as part of the experience. The program is offered between the months of June and September each year. What a great way to spend some quality time with the family while enjoying the outdoor lives of our animal friends. On our visit to the zoo, we couldn't enjoy seeing all of the hundreds of animals that are meticulously housed there, but we did get to see *Mei Xiang* and *Tian*, the two panda residents (*Mei Xiang* gave birth to *Tai Shan* in 2005). We also had the opportunity to walk the Asia Trail, which has a series of habitats for seven Asian species, including sloth bears, red pandas, and clouded leopards. Another thrill we enjoyed with our children, no grandchildren allowed, was the "Brew at the Zoo" beer sampling from the microbreweries located at the zoo; it worked wonders in cooling us off on the hot day that we visited.

It is a beautiful, free-of-charge urban family park with something new to discover at every twist and turn throughout the animal kingdom. The zoo has a long history of innovation and leadership in the care of wild animal exhibitions that also includes educational and scientific programs, both on-site and around the world. Some of the popular programs are:

- **Woo at the Zoo** – A Valentine's Day talk by some of the zoo's animal experts discussing the fascinating, and often quirky, world of animal dating, mating, and reproductive habits.
- **Earth Day – Party for the Planet** – A celebration of Earth Day, where guests can find out about simple daily actions they can take to enjoy a more environmentally friendly lifestyle.
- **Easter Monday** – Easter Monday has been a Washington-area multicultural tradition for many years. There is a variety of family activities, entertainment, and special opportunities to learn more about animals. The celebration began in response to the inability of African Americans to participate in the annual Easter Egg Roll held on the White House lawn prior to Dwight Eisenhower's presidency.
- **Zoofari** – A casual evening of gourmet foods, fine wines, entertainment, and dancing under the stars. Each year, thousands of attendees enjoy delicacies prepared by master chefs from a hundred of the DC area's finest restaurants.
- **Zoolights** – Is the National Zoo's annual winter celebration. Guests can walk through the zoo when it is covered with thousands of sparkling, environmentally friendly lights and animated exhibits, attend special keeper talks, and enjoy live evening entertainment.

Almost all of the above mentioned venues are available, free of charge, due to the thousands of volunteers—many of whom are seniors—that devote their precious time for the betterment of the millions of visitors to our country's capital.

Other vacations that we were fortunate to enjoy and remove, one by one, from our *Bucket List*, were visits to our National Parks: Yellowstone, Grand Canyon, Bryce, Zion, Yosemite, Redwood Forest, and Mount Rushmore. We have traveled and spent time in Italy (four times), France, England, Greece, Switzerland, Argentina, Nova Scotia, Alaska, Niagara Falls, and Quebec and Montreal, in Canada. We have sailed the Caribbean several times, visiting her many islands along the way; we've sailed the Mediterranean visiting Greece and its treasured islands of Santorini and Mykonos; Kusadasi and Istanbul in Turkey, and Venice, Sicily and Sardinia in Italy. We have also sailed from England to the Baltic Countries visiting Norway, Sweden, Denmark, Estonia, Finland, and Russia. We have sailed and visited the Islands of Hawaii (three times), and have sailed on our boats to Montauk Point, Long Island; Martha's Vineyard, Nantucket, New Bedford, Plymouth, and Cape Cod in Massachusetts; Block Island, Newport and Narragansett Bay and surrounding islands, in Rhode Island; and Essex, East Norwich, Cedar, and the Thimble Island in Connecticut. New Year's Eve, 2012, we sailed on the largest cruise liner in the world, the *Allure of the Seas*, to many of the Caribbean Islands for a week of fun and sunshine on a ship that spared no costs to entertain their passengers, with onboard Zip Lines, astonishing Aqua Shows, an ice skating rink that converted to a ballroom dance floor, and a basketball court. The "cream of the trip" was a day on their private pristine island of Labadee, Haiti, where swimming, sunning, zip lining, parasailing, fishing, an endless BBQ, and on and on.

As we are celebrating our 50th wedding anniversary in September, 2014, we booked a cruise on the *Queen Mary 2* to celebrate the event. The 12 day cruise will leave from the Brooklyn, NY, piers and travel to Newport, RI; Boston, MA; Bar Harbor, ME; St. John, NB; Halifax, NS, and Quebec, Canada. The grand lady will disembark at one of the Manhattan piers in New York City. The ship boasts of having the largest ballroom dance floor at sea. Our formal clothes, which are required wear on many of the evenings, are ready and hopefully will still fit our ancient bodies. Whatever the case may be, it promises to be an exciting and memorable golden anniversary party for us. Two ballroom dance groups that we are familiar with are also voyaging on her majesty, so the 12 days should be filled with fun and lots of dancing with some old friends, and I know, many new acquaintances.

CHAPTER FIVE

Part-Time Jobs for Retirees

The employee Benefit Research Institute's 2013 Retirement Confidence Survey, which is a "state of retirement planning document" that comes out each year, makes it clear that many seniors will have no choice but to enter the part-time job market to accomplish some degree of financial independence during their retirement. Some of the highlights of their report were surprising:

- 57 percent of workers surveyed have less than $25,000 in savings and investments.
- More than half of the workers have not tried to determine how much money they will need for retirement.
- Only 14 percent of the workers are very confident in their ability to retire comfortably.

Whether your needs are financial or you simply enjoy having a place to go to every day to mingle with coworkers, being employed on a part time basis after retirement can be a smart decision, and—as the above survey indicates—in many cases, a necessity. But continuing to work doesn't necessarily condemn you to a 9-to-5 grind.

Prior generations were not as fortunate as we are today, as most people did not live past 65. Now, one in eight Americans is 65 or older, with an average life expectancy of 84. As we can see, many people will have to support themselves for longer periods of time by either remaining in the workforce longer or by working part time to supplement their finances.

Some of my friends have combined part-time jobs with pleasure. Cruise ships have offered them an opportunity to earn pocket money while traveling around the world. The ships provide room and board and the use of their facilities when the workers are not plying their trade. In many cases, the retirees escort tour guides on sightseeing trips, which gives them an opportunity to travel and explore in style at no charge. Some of the job openings, descriptions, and requirements that cruise lines use for hiring aboard their ships are as follows:

- **Golf Instructors**—the job entails operating golf simulators, playing golf with passengers, and other cruise staff duties; the instructors must be fluent in English. These positions call for very independent individuals who have the capacity and patience to teach at all levels of the game and must have the ability to interact in social situations with the cruise line's guests and staff personnel. They must also possess the motivation and business acumen to operate an on-board operation in its entirety, including self-promotion and instruction, and must also assist with shore excursions.

- **Scuba Diving/Water Sports Instructors**—they conduct daily diving and snorkeling programs and meticulously maintain equipment. A diving instructor's certificate, and Cardiopulmonary Resuscitation (CPR) and First Aid certificates are required.

- **Bridge Instructors**—must be experienced bridge teachers and ACBL-certified directors who have achieved "Life Masters" standing. The directors must be proficient at both Standard American and ACOL and must be excellent socializers with outgoing, dynamic personalities. The directors will be responsible for teaching bridge to intermediate and advanced players, followed by afternoons of duplicate and social bridge play on each day the ship is at sea and on select port days. Depending on the ship, the instructors may also be asked to offer lessons to absolute beginners. The bridge instructors will also be responsible for submitting any master points earned by passengers who are members of the ACBL.

- **Texas 42 Instructors**—often referred to as "the National Game of Texas." It's a popular domino game similar in strategy to the card game of bridge, but not as complicated. Experts of the game will teach passengers how to play and improve their games and will host game plays on each sea day. The instructors must be friendly, flexible, and excellent socializers with outgoing, dynamic personalities. The instructors will be responsible for teaching lessons to absolute beginners and intermediate and advanced players. Lessons are followed by game plays on each of the days that the ship is at sea and on select port days. The instructors will also be responsible for consumable supplies, such as dominos, pads of paper, and pens.

- **Arts and Craft Instructors**—they must be friendly, patient, and creative and enjoy teaching craft projects to the guests. The instructors will be responsible for providing the supplies needed to make the crafts and must prepare an original project for each class. Examples of craft lessons may include "The Joy of Scrapbooking," "Easy-to-Make Christmas Ornaments," or "The Art of Watercolor."

- **Caricature Artists**—they serve as part of the ship's enrichment staff. Everyone loves to bring home a fun, visual memory of their cruise vacation, which is why the artists are so popular aboard ships. During a cruise assignment, a Caricaturist's responsibilities include quick and fun drawings, which are offered at no charge to passengers. Usually, Caricaturists are located in popular high traffic areas of the ship where they sketch individuals, as well as groups of family and friends traveling together. As a general rule of thumb, less than five minutes should be spent on each drawing. The artists must be friendly, creative, and have excellent social skills.

- **Dance Instructors**—should apply as a couple and must be proficient in all dance styles—from the classics to the current fads—and offer lessons to passengers of all ages and abilities.

One day might feature lessons on traditional ballroom dance techniques, including Waltz and the Foxtrot, while the next might be spent teaching line dancing or the Macarena. Dance instructors must be outgoing, friendly, and prepared for any unusual situations on the dance floors, such as students falling or losing their balance. They may also be asked to assist with shore excursions. Some ships allow instructors to give private lessons and pocket the money. Certainly a great way to earn money while enjoying one's self.

- **Dance Hosts**—must know how to dance most of the above named dances and must be personable, clean, and above all, friendly. On many cruise ships, they are required to have formal dress wear.
- **Photography**—persons should be proficient in camera equipment and excellent in photograph setups. Must be self-starters and extremely polite and professional in dealing with passengers.
- **Lecturers**—must have credentials in their field of expertise, such as professors, authors, and persons of renown.

The opportunities for part-time work on cruise ships are endless. Where else can retirees spend time teaching what they enjoy, while traveling around the world and eating wonderful food and also, where the opportunity is available, earning extra pocket money? I have a friend that has been a dance host on ships for the last six years, and plans on continuing for as long as his legs hold out. The amazing thing about him is that he has managed to maintain his weight, considering the availability of the tempting food on large cruise ships. If anyone is interested, it's easy to find job openings by accessing cruise lines' websites.

Of the many part-time opportunities, some of the more popular that combine flexible working hours with pleasure for retirees are the following:

- **Librarians**—the duties include answering customers' questions, shelving books, helping patrons check out books, tracking overdue material, and sending notices, as well as cataloging and keeping an eye out for lost and damaged items.

- **Bookkeepers**—usually the opportunities are with small businesses and entail a full sweep of financial recordkeeping. Some of the duties may include establishing and maintaining inventory database systems, tracing accounts receivable and accounts payable, maintaining checking and savings accounts, producing financial reports, following up on delinquent accounts, and assisting in audits and reviews. Needless to say, this type of work requires previous experience in bookkeeping and computer applications. The old method of handwritten information data entry is rapidly disappearing, so it's essential to be familiar with computer bookkeeping to secure this type of position.

- **Personal and Home Care Aides**—this type of work typically includes caring for the elderly, ill, or disabled with everyday activities ranging from bathing and getting dressed to running errands. Other duties might include light housekeeping, companionship, grocery shopping, meal preparation, and medication monitoring.

For those who prefer working at home, there are many opportunities available. Of course, some of the advantages are working in a familiar surroundings and no longer having to commute or deal with annoying co-workers. Working at home certainly has a nice ring to it—sometimes too nice. **Work-at-home scams** are something that must be kept in mind when considering allowing your home to be used for someone else's business. The Federal Trade Commission (FTC) states that the number of scams reported have doubled over last year. Two glaring red flags to look for are: jobs touted via email that promise to pay "more than you've ever dreamed of," and firms that charge a fee for you to obtain more information about a job or that require paying for supplies. "Payment for the privilege of working is rarely acceptable, in our view," says Christine Durst, an Internet fraud and safety expert and co-founder of www.ratracerebellion.com, a website dedicated to home-based work. It screens job leads for at-home work.

That being said, there are certainly many legitimate at-home jobs waiting to be filled by seniors, but checking them out for scams is imperative. Some nice, safe job opportunities are:

- **Customer Service Representatives**—It is surprising how many overseas jobs have returned to the United States from India, the Philippines, and other offshore locations in this field. Many companies such as Home Depot, Hilton Hotels, American Airlines, and 1-800-Flowers hire representatives directly, but there is a growing market for "**virtual call center operators.**" One of the largest is Alpine Access at www.alpineaccess.com, which is headquartered in Denver and has over 4,500 part-time, at-home employees in 1,700 cities across the United States. Those applying for the jobs must have an up-to-date computer, a high-speed Internet connection, a dedicated land line, a telephone headset, and a quiet place to work. In general, they answer incoming calls for companies, take orders, track existing orders, and in some cases troubleshoot and help out with technical support. Some of the advantages of this type of at-home work are flexible hours, lucrative hourly wages, and, in many cases, vacations and fringe benefits. In addition to Alpine, other virtual call center operators' websites include www.liveops.com, www.westathome.com, and www. workingsolutions.com. It is estimated that over 50,000 –people are employed in the U.S. as operators; the number is growing as our citizens continue to complain about their difficulties with understanding the foreign accents of outsourced workers, and their displeasure with American jobs going overseas.
- **Virtual Assistants**—the main purpose of these positions is to assist busy business executives who do not have in-house staff to attend to various administrative functions. These positions have become available due to small companies trying to keep permanent overhead costs down. Training programs are available at community colleges, many of which offer online certifications. The duties of an assistant range from making traveling arrangements to sending out letters and

other support services, which are easily handled remotely via email and telephone. Job openings can be explored at www.virtualassistantjobs.com and at www.teamdoubleclick.com.

- **Online Tutoring**—private online tutoring sessions with students is a growing job market due to the super-competitive college admissions programs. The subjects in demand are the core topics: world history, physics, science, mathematics, and English. Foreign languages especially are seeing an increase in demand for this kind of service. An online employer at www.tutor.com offers one-on-one help to students and is set up so that when students need help with their homework, they enter their grade level and subject of interest into their computer log-on screen. Based on the information, an appropriate tutor (the firm has over two thousand on board) is assigned and a relationship is born. Some other tutoring firms with job openings are found at www.kaplan.com and www.Smarthinking.com.

In the part-time job market, some of the most exciting opportunities have become available for snowbirds. With more and more seniors flying to Florida and Arizona during the cold winter months, jobs in preferred winter states are plentiful and require only a little or no experience. For instance, Disney in Florida and California have jobs openings that run the gamut from dressing as a member of the mouse family to escorting tourists around the vast entertainment facilities. Some of the available jobs in both resorts are: loading and unloading passengers from rides, doling out costumes at wardrobe facilities across the parks, staffing gift shops and concessions, and being costumed cast members throughout the parks. For those who like being around airplanes, there are also openings for airport representatives who greet guests at arrival and usher them to waiting shuttles. Of course, there are many opportunities for responsible seniors in the resorts transportation departments, as older and wiser drivers are preferred to younger and somewhat carefree drivers. Checking the Walt Disney World website for job openings and qualifications is easily accomplished for anyone that "Believes in magic," and loves dealing with children aged from one to ninety.

Disney doesn't have a monopoly on seasonal employment opportunities at resorts. All kinds of jobs become available across the Sunbelt when snowbirds flock down South. Jobs ranging from bartenders or gardeners to parking valets and room cleaners are in demand during the winter season, at very lucrative pay rates. If a senior loves golf or tennis, there might be openings in pro shops or as a caddy or ball retriever. Gambling fans should investigate casinos, and boating enthusiasts can find many job openings at marinas.

For those that have good eyesight, a valid driver's license, and enjoy the open road, delivering cars up and down the East Coast can pay very nicely, while picking up frequent flyer miles on the return trips. The busiest months are December and May, but departures and returns are ongoing, though at a reduced salary between non-peak months. These jobs can net a driver up to $200 per day, with all costs paid, including service to airports and air flights on return trips.

To emphasize that dreams can come true in our golden years, I know someone who is a diehard baseball fan that was able to get a job at a spring training camp for a Major League Baseball team. This relatively quiet person has become the most gregarious person I know and can't stop talking about the fun and satisfaction he gets from being around baseball stars and fans. Some job openings are: ushering fans to their seats, selling programs, fielding ticket inquiries, working concession booths, and driving players and staff to and from airports. There are also many job opportunities with the teams for seniors with experience in sales as seasonal assistants, helping in marketing and special promotions. Former Information Technicians can usually find seasonal work making sure wireless networks and computers run smoothly for the press and players. While duties might be routine, the chance to rub shoulders with a World Series ring bearer is certainly a dream come true for any baseball fan. A good place to find job openings is the Major League Baseball's website; click on the link to your favorite baseball team, then click on "job opportunities," and if you are one of the lucky ones, you'll be on your way to having a **dream come true.**

An interesting article appeared in the Florida Sun Sentinel on May 3, 2013 under the headline of **Hundreds Turn Out for Dolphin's Job Fair:**

Hundreds of South Floridians showed up at the Sun Life Stadium on Thursday for what the Miami Dolphins dubbed an 'opportunity fair' for job seekers interested in helping modernize the venue. South Florida Workforce, the agency helping identify the workers, said 590 people stopped by.

The Dolphins' organization said it needs to upgrade the stadium to make it a top contender for Super Bowls and other national events. The $350 million plan still needs approval from lawmakers and Miami-Dade County voters.

Someone drove from as far away as Deerfield Beach to the Miami Gardens Stadium, excited about the possibility of a job that would support the Dolphins' vision. 'I want to be a part of it in some small way,' the **63-year**-old Dolphins fan said. 'Other cities have great stadiums. I think we should have the best one of all.'

Aside from the modernization-related opportunity, about **700 seasonal jobs** for stadium events were available Thursday, said the human resources executive for the Dolphins. Within the first hour of the four hour event, 116 people had inquired about those positions, she said.

A Fort Lauderdale resident said that she would like to work as one of the gate attendants, collecting tickets from the event-goers. She also picked up a flyer on constructions jobs, just in case she couldn't get her dream job, anything to be around her beloved football team. She said 'I don't do construction, but if that's all they have, I'll gladly take it.'

The above article is an example of the opportunities that exist for retirees seeking part-time employment; all that is required is looking around, first for jobs that you have a passion for, and if you're not successful in those, there are certainly a multitude of other opportunities that can put extra money into your pocketbook.

Financial Considerations

Much of my writing, so far, has been related to the fun things that concern retirees. It is appropriate now to delve into the not-so-happy topics, those that possibly require changing how we think and our capacity to try to anticipate our future in a financial and physical way. It's important that we develop a **roadmap** to our retirement so that when the time comes we are prepared, in the best possible way, to have a strategy to follow that will lead us to financial and physical success. I found that using modern technology and information that was readily available made our retirement years more fruitful and allowed us to be independent, which was of the utmost importance. Following are some of the strategies that made Barbara and I enjoy our golden years with as little stress from paperwork as possible and lots of time to do the fun things that we always dreamed about.

Computer Assistance

Where do we begin when discussing computer technology and how it impacts our everyday lives, whether through laptops, desktops, iPods, telephones, or the multitude of other applications that are computer software based? In the year 2000, I wrote a book, *Business Infrastructure in a Computer Environment.* At that time, personal computers were in an experimental stage, with users exploring their usefulness in the commercial and personal markets. As a matter of fact, IBM gave away most of its rights to personal computer software development as it was convinced that the **small babies** would be a distraction from their profitable, large mainframe computer markets. They, in effect, restricted the sales of their personal computers to a handful of resellers, thereby limiting their market and allowing an opening for other manufacturers such as Epson, Panasonic, H.P., and Dell to surpass them in the personal computer marketplace. Their thinking, unfortunately, has carried over into the minds of many people who still believe that personal computers have no place in their lives or who refuse to experiment with this amazing technology. A copy of the covers of my book *Business Infrastructure in a Computer Environment* follows:

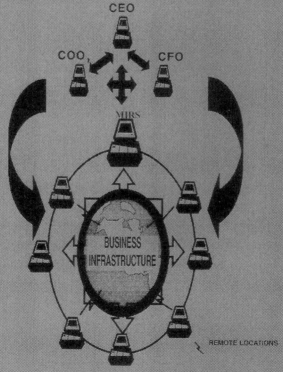

Within the structure of today's increasingly complex corporate world, author Michael Bivona's *Business Infrastructure: In a Computer Environment* is a blueprint for success.

As technology and finance shape tomorrow's companies, organizational issues become more and more crucial. The author's analysis clearly shows how wise development can translate into increased profits and productivity. The complexities of infrastructure are examined with regard to internal operations, such as customer service departments.

This is a book that is certain to be welcomed by managers and supervisors in large and small firms; and a must for young people starting out in the business world.

Many seniors, although they are well versed and wouldn't be caught dead without a smartphone, are reluctant to experiment with a computer mouse or keyboard, and seem to avoid contact with PCs at any cost, probably because they are intimidated by the keyboard and fear that they are not capable of mastering the equipment. From my many enquiries, it seems that even if they do own a PC, they prefer not to us them when it comes to paying bills or exposing themselves to the dangers that seems to have perpetuated the internet, such as viruses and the hacking of personal information.

I did some random sampling to determine what Baby Boomers, people born after WW2, used to pay bills and to keep track of important information that will be relevant in making their retirement planning easier. I was surprised to find that many Boomers that were already retired still paid their bills by hand-written checks and the use of the mail, and had no idea of how important keeping track of their financial information in a convenient place, like a PC, was to their future financial wellbeing. Many Boomers that were nearing retirement, I found, paid many of their bills with the same monthly amounts through automatic withdrawals from their banks and the balance by hand-written checks. As the Boomers I interviewed got younger, many seemed to favor paying their bills using tablets and smartphones, and many didn't give too much thought as to how the equipment would help them with their retirement planning. Hacking personal information seemed to be of little concern to many of the younger people that I interviewed. I was also surprised that many Boomers that used tablets and smartphones to pay their bills, relied on their electronic equipment to keep them posted as to what their bank balances were, without checking the details or accuracy of their accounts on an ongoing basis.

Today's computer technology already has an impact on almost every facet of our lives. There are different kinds of computers, other than the personal ones, that help us in more ways than we realize. There are basically four kinds that impact our lives in different ways, in different places and for different purposes. So, what are they, and how do they affect our lives?

- **Personal Computers**—these are used by one person at a time and are probably found on desktops in a majority of homes in the United States and other first-world countries. Many have additional microprocessors so that they can perform special tasks like graphics, math, sounds, etc. They are also used in businesses, and have many features that help with simple to complicated tasks. These tasks may include word-processing, storing information in a file, researching subjects, etc. They can also be used for educational purposes, leisure (games), listening to music, watching movies, Skype, email, accessing the Internet, and much more. Under this type there are desktops, laptops, notebook computers, tablets, and all other kinds of Personal Digital Assistants (PDAs), and smartphones.
- **Mainframes**—this type of computer is the fastest of them all. These are significantly larger than their little sisters with some having almost infinite storage capacities. Some

mainframes may have hundreds or more people at the same time accessing their intelligence and sharing information. Supercomputers, the fastest of the mainframes, are used to do even more complex projects like designing aircraft or building skyscrapers. These computers are primarily used for commercial and government purposes and can cost millions of dollars.

- **Dedicated Computers**—these are special-purpose machines. Some examples are word processors and video-game units. The smallest of the video-game units are battery-operated ones such as Gameboy. Larger ones are plug-ins into televisions like Xbox and PlayStation. The largest of these are found in game arcades and gambling casinos.
- **Embedded Computers**—these are control units built into the devices they control. Examples are telephones, digital watches, and VCRs. Aircraft and robots also have embedded computers, while guided missiles use them to find their targets.

So as we can see, many of us, although we might not own or use personal computers, do use computer technology in our everyday lives. As a matter of fact, who of us hasn't watched the weather reports on television and enjoyed the information that was derived from mainframes connected throughout the world? Who of us hasn't played with video games, if not our own then with those of our grandchildren? Who of us hasn't taken their grandchildren to an arcade and joined them in playing with the amazing games that light up the environment and increase the noise level beyond one's tolerance?

Considering that we are dependent on computers in our everyday lives without owning or actually using them, I think the next logical step for those who do not possess the magical machines should be to go out and buy one. Well, what does all this have to do with making life a little more intellectual and interesting during retirement? Remember the article by Professor Richard Powers, "Use it or Lose it," that I wrote about previously? According to Professor Powers, "the more new things we learn the more building blocks get added to our brain; the more building blocks added to our brain the longer our intellectual awareness will prevail."

When it comes to learning new things, I can't think of a better place than in your home maneuvering through a personal computer and exploring the infinite possibilities for intellectual growth. Again, you may ask, what does this have to do with senior citizens? The answer is obvious: at that time of life when our brains begin to play tricks on us, what better way to forestall the inevitable then to force new brain cells to develop in our minds? An example of increasing our prowess with the use of PCs is to access the internet and have fun at the same time by using applications such as Skype to see and talk to our grandchildren and our friends. This is accomplished by having cameras attached to personal computers that allow people to see and converse with each other free of charge; many laptops today come with built-in cameras. In our case, we had a new grandson Michael who was born on October 1, 2010 in Atlanta, Ga. We live on Long Island, NY and Delray Beach, FL, and communicate with our daughter and her son several times a week, so we can watch our baby make sounds and take baths without being with him, but certainly enjoying his experience as if we were there. Facebook is another fun computer application through which people can keep in touch with family and friends, at no charge, over the internet. It seems that today the only way to keep in touch with the young people in our lives on an ongoing basis is to participate with them in their love affair with Facebook.

Again, what does owning a computer have to do with retirement plans? The reality is that it makes life a lot easier, as I found in my case. I'm not as patient as I was in days-gone-by and find it a lot easier to use the Internet to get information, buy products, and deal with companies than I did by calling on the telephone or shopping at stores. In addition, travel information, movie schedules and reviews, and restaurants and their menus are at your fingertips as well as most other information that you might need. The bottom line is it makes us more **self-sufficient** at a time in life when we're expected to be more dependent on others for many of our needs. As previously mentioned, the many job opportunities that are available to seniors can easily be accessed if a computer is at hand. The advantages are endless, especially when trying to decide where to spend our retirement years without having to travel to faraway places to investigate for ourselves. Today, one can use virtual reality applications to actually see houses and their contents, get pricing information, travel through neighborhoods, and finally, only actually visiting those places that look like possible retirement communities; all this can be done without wasting time traveling around the country. What an amazing time-saver at that point in our lives when time is so precious and running out at what seems to be an accelerated pace.

We shouldn't discount the importance of computer use in the financial activities that seem to become more burdensome in our senior years. Especially useful is the reduction in record keeping, more so for those of us who are snowbirds. When we became members of the winged family about 14 years ago, I was overwhelmed with writing duplicate monthly checks for our telephone, electricity, insurance, heat, air conditioning, mortgage payments, and my other miscellaneous bills. Living in two locations compounded the dreaded task of paying additional monthly bills that included snow removal, which I used to do myself when I spent the white months in New York, and house-sitting bills for winter and summer house sitters. Keeping track of bills, paying them manually with hand-written checks, inserting the bills and payments into envelopes after addressing them, and finally after stamping the envelopes and posting them at the most convenient mail drop became an overwhelming task. Making sure that all of my bills were paid promptly became a "pain-in-the-butt" due to the multitude and the different times that bills had to be paid. A nightmare was when there were disputes with creditors; especially irritating was proving that bills were paid on time and trying to explain to creditors why they hadn't receive the payment or why it was received late, which invariably would result in late payment charges and lots of aggravation and wasted time.

What to do? Considering that I was retired from the computer industry, one would assume that I would have paid my bills with the help of a computer over the Internet long before retiring. Well, I guess I'm as guilty as the next person when it comes to using a PC to break old habits. Out of desperation, I went to my bank and told them that they must come up with a better method for me to satisfy my obligations before I went crazy trying to keep up with the ever-growing stack of paperwork. Their answer was quite clear; they had a better method, at no charge, and began indoctrinating me in all the reasons why I should be paying my bills from my PC keyboard instead of handwriting them from my checkbook. It didn't take too long for me to appreciate the advantages of not having to write checks manually, of not having to insert bills into envelopes, of not having to address envelopes, of not having to buy and place stamps on envelopes, and then finally posting the mail. Just the savings on postage stamps, which seemed to be increasing in price every year, was worth changing my life-long habit of doing things by hand and in a familiar way.

I know that many retirees already use computers to pay their bills. Some even have telephone payments set up with their banks or even have direct payment withdrawals from their checking accounts. If a person doesn't have too many bills to pay, telephone payments can be an option rather than using a computer, but it's not as efficient and requires accumulating bills and calling several times a month to have timely payments made. For those who have direct withdrawals, I give them credit for being very trusting; I'm never comfortable with having money withdrawn from my bank accounts by vendors, automatically, without my first reviewing bills, and it certainly becomes very frustrating resolving bill disputes with creditors over the phone after a bill is paid—that is, if you can find a person on the other end that understands English.

For those who don't use the telephone or direct withdrawal methods, or who wish to change, I'm going to go through the steps that led me to being a less stressed person in my senior years by eliminating a task that I detested. My first step was to set up a creditor list for my monthly payments for telephone bills, electric bills, garbage collection, car payments, mortgage payments, etc., by name, address, and my customer numbers. **How sweet it was** when I paid my first series of bills without having to touch my checkbook. I selected the creditors that I wanted to pay, they appeared one by one on my computer screen, I inserted the dollar amounts and the dates that I wanted the bank to make payments, and *voila*, electronic instructions to the bank were written in "computer stone." One major advantage that I noticed right away was that if the payee had what is known as "Electronic Transfers," I was able to set up a payment for two days prior to the due date and not worry about the payment ever being late, as I had proof at my fingertips as to when my bank transferred the funds directly into the payee's account. Next, I set up automatic recurring payments for automobiles, mortgages, insurance, and association fees; being that the payments are for the same amounts each time, it was easy to schedule them for monthly, quarterly, or whatever timeframe was necessary to satisfy the obligation. **Bingo!** After setting up my scheduled payments, the bank honored my payment requests without missing a beat and, at stipulated time periods, issued checks or electronic transfers to the payees without my getting involved. After my computerized payment method became routine, I felt the stress of my monthly bill-paying nightmare disappear. A major bonus was that if I wanted to know if a bill had been paid and the date it cleared the creditor's bank, by the touch of the proper keys on my PC, I could access the information and had the ability to send a copy of the check or electronic information to anyone that claimed a payment wasn't received. Another bonus is that there are no more checks to store, as the bank keeps all the records in their electronic files. A really sweet feature is that if a payment is missed, whether it's because a bill wasn't received or just plain forgotten, a procedure is available to remind you that a payment that was scheduled wasn't made.

An efficient time saver for me was when paying subsequent bills. If payments were not on my "Recurring List," which meant they would be paid automatically, when preparing to pay a current bill, the last payment date and amount appeared on the screen next to the current information that is being input into the computer. This helps to determine if a previous payment was missed, or if the current bill is out of line with a prior payment, or if the bill is a duplicate. Another great feature is that the amounts paid to individual vendors are accumulated and at any given moment how much was paid to each is easily determined. This is especially useful when planning future spending budgets and in determining how much money is needed during retirement years to live comfortably.

Computerized banking almost forces people to check their bank accounts frequently to make sure that payments are made as scheduled and that deposits are recorded correctly. You go from being an active player to an overseer; your main purpose is to make sure that your instructions have been followed correctly. I check my account almost every day, which makes me aware of my financial obligations and status. It is imperative that seniors control their own finances as long as they are able, and keeping an eye on our bank accounts frequently is certainly one way of accomplishing that, rather than on a monthly basis when a printed statement is delivered to our home by mail with information that is well after the fact and the bank transactions are far from our thoughts or concern. Another thing to keep in mind is that a laptop computer, and there are many small ones available, can be taken with you wherever you travel, and accessing the Internet with today's high-speed routers and Wi Fi makes the experience of paying bills and getting other important information a pleasant one when away from the comfort of your home. When we are on the road for extended periods of time, I call vendors to determine how much I owe them or, where the opportunity is available, I access my account on the creditor's website and then pay my bills from the data from those sources. Of course, today, the same results can be accomplished with the use of iPads, iPods and a number of other pocket sized electronic devices, but that is a topic for another day, but the theory is the same.

Unfortunately, as time goes by, seniors may not have the wherewithal to continue handling their own finances efficiently. I can best explain the importance of computerized banking for some people by using an example of when we cared for a relative that was disabled and not capable of handling her finances. She lived in Florida; we were located in New York, so tending to her financial needs in person was not feasible. Putting the relative in a nursing home was not an option, so we arranged for in-home care with a group of professionals to attend to her needs. They rotated shifts and made sure that the necessary care was provided around the clock. Now the question of paying household bills and the caretakers' fees became a problem as we were not nearby to monitor firsthand what was going on in Florida. So what we did was open a bank account for her and linked it to our checking account. By doing this, we were able to keep track on our PC of the amount of funds that was necessary every month to pay bills and would transfer the necessary sums into her account by pressing a few keys on our computer. In addition to making cash transfers easy, we were able to see the back and front of checks that the caretaker responsible for paying bills issued for the benefit of our relative. Of course, we made several visits a year to Florida to spend time with her and to keep in touch with the people in the network that were caring for our loved one. In our case, a computer made a difficult situation manageable and she was able to spend her remaining days on earth in her home, as she had wished.

Most seniors use direct bank deposits for their monthly social security checks. Many may even use the direct deposit method for their pension incomes. But what about other income that is received through the mail and requires preparing a deposit slip and a visit to a local bank, such as dividends earned, annuity checks, interest income, and other repetitive sums that are received on a regular basis in the form of a check that must be deposited or mailed to the recipient's bank? I'd like to list some of the advantages of direct deposits for those who are skeptical about losing control of their deposits if they don't receive a piece of paper, and that's all that it is, a piece of paper:

- There are no checks to get lost or stolen.
- Income payments reach bank accounts on the day they are issued, regardless of whether you are out of town or sick.
- Many banks offer free or lower-cost checking to customers with direct deposits because it saves them the cost of processing paper checks.
- Direct deposits can help prevent you from bouncing checks as the deposits are recorded on the day issued.
- It saves trips to the bank and helps avoid the usual long lines at the teller's window.

For seniors that are disabled or unable to get to a bank to make deposits, establishing a direct system is a "God-send," because:

- With the use of a PC, you can determine if the deposits were recorded on time and plan payments accordingly.
- Guess what? You don't have to keep a checkbook balance; the information is at your fingertips at the keyboard.

Online banking can be a senior citizen's best friend; after trying it, you'll wonder how you lived without it for so long and maintained your sanity. With online banking, most of your financial life is in one neat "virtual" place with access 24/7 from the comfort of your home. This is especially convenient for those who can no longer drive, are disabled, or have arthritic fingers and find it difficult to write checks legibly. Bills can be paid day or night with just a few clicks on a keyboard, and reviewing your account statement to determine if bills were paid and to keep apprised of account balances becomes routine and sets the stage for proper budgeting of retirement funds.

If you are comfortable with e-bill payments, many companies offer the option of having you sign up for their automatic deductions from your bank account of current bills such as telephone, electric, insurance, association fees, garbage removal, etc. This puts you in a position of supervising your bill payments instead of getting involved with their payments. With online banking, including direct deposits, in your life, determining how stable your finances are for retirement becomes a "no brainer." With a little ingenuity, eliminating or reducing expenses that are no longer necessary and forecasting how much money we should transfer into our checking accounts from our savings accounts to live comfortably is reduced to a manageable task that most people are able to handle with ease. If a person is not comfortable about doing the arithmetic, the information is readily available from the computer to seek out a reputable financial advisor to discuss budgeting based on the data that have been accumulated over the years.

An ongoing problem for seniors is identity thefts. Owning a PC can, in many ways, avoid the creative ways that thieves are using to steal money from the public, especially senior citizens, who, as they age, seem to become lax in checking their financial and personal records.

Identity Theft

In 2013, over 16 million households fell victim to identity theft at a great cost of money, time, and unwelcomed stress. According to Javelin Strategy & Research, a Greenwich Associates, LLC Company that provides insight into customer transactions, there was a new victim of identity fraud every two seconds in 2013.

From my experience as an accountant and financial advisor, I've learned some of the ways to reduce the risk of loss, especially for seniors who seem to be major targets for thieves, such as:

- Enroll for free alerts from your bank and credit card issuers to flag unusual activity on your accounts. Or, if you have a PC, check your bank and credit card balances several times a week. It doesn't take but a few minutes to determine if an unusual item has made its way into your accounts.
- Remove your name from mailing lists for preapproved credit card offers, which seems to be a goldmine for identity thieves. Call 888-567-8688 to block information about your name. Also, stop other junk mail by going to www.dmachoice.org and follow instructions on their website.
- Request your credit card providers to issue new "smart cards" for MasterCard, Visa, or any other credit card, with new chip technology. Also, where available, have photo credit cards issued.
- To protect personal data on electronic devices, change passwords frequently and try to mix letters and numbers. Don't use 1234, 0000, 1111 or repetitive numbers on computers, smartphones, or charge accounts; these types of numbers make it easy for hackers to access personal documents and information.
- Several times a year, access the free credit reports at www.annualcreditreport.com to determine who has been requesting information about your credit.
- If you're not planning to apply for new credit, loans, insurance, or utility services, freeze your report so thieves can't get information that might be necessary to open accounts in your

name. Although states have different rules about blocking information, it's worth a try to block personal information, as fees are often waived for seniors 65 or older or if a person can prove that there has been a prior identity theft. Type "Security Freeze" at the websites of Experian, Equifax, and TransUnion for instruction on how to proceed.

- For those who still pay their bills by regular mail, try to go to the nearest post office to mail payments, rather than from the more defenseless home mailboxes.

- Always shred documents that contain personal information before disposing of them. If a shredder is not available, then tear important documents in different directions to limit the possibility of crooks reconstructing sensitive information.

- Find out if your Internet provider offers free antivirus software. Set it for automatic security updates and full scans. If free service is not available, purchase antivirus software from McAfee, Norton, Kaspersky, or other legitimate organizations providing that service. It's relatively cheap and for one price many companies offer coverage for up to three computers. I just installed Kaspersky on three computers for two years at a cost of $99.

- Avoid clicking on links in emails from people you don't know, or from government agencies or a bank warning of a problem. They are probably identity-theft malware that will install on your computer, resulting in all sorts of grief.

- Don't carry your Medicare card with you unless you're going to a doctor's office; the number is the same as your Social Security number. If necessary, you'll get emergency medical treatment without it, or if you're concerned, carry a photocopy with some digits missing. Carry your Social Security card only for visits to Social Security offices.

- Never provide personal information, including your Social Security number, to anyone unless you initiate the contact.

- If you subscribe to Facebook or similar sites, make sure you limit your personal information, as these are hunting grounds for identity thieves.

- Credit and debit cards have also become targets of ID thieves. If an unauthorized person goes on a shopping spree with a stolen credit card, the liability to the owner is limited to $50.00, and assistance is forthwith from the credit card company in handling fraudulent charges. But, if debit card information is stolen and fraudulent charges are made to the account, consumers who wait more than two days to report the theft could be responsible for up to $500 for illegal charges. If the fraudulent activity goes unreported for 60 days after receiving the statement with the fraudulent charges, there is a risk of losing even more.

In April of 2014, Senator Mark Warner of Virginia and Senator Mark Kirk of Illinois introduced a bill proposing that debit cards have the same $50 liability cap as credit cards for unauthorized activity.

As we can see, it's important to become proactive when it comes to preventing identity theft, and having a personal computer and checking bank accounts and credit card activity frequently can save lots of money and *mucho* grief if there is an unfortunate breach in how we handle our finances.

How Important are Social Security Benefits?

A successful and fulfilling retirement means different things to different folks. It may mean going from a full-time career into part-time work or spending more time with family and friends, or starting a garden, or making regular visits to tennis courts or golf courses. Once the decision is made as to what may make you happy in retirement, it's important to know how to get there financially. The first step is to write your objectives down, listing the most important goals first without considering the cost. Try to concentrate on the top five important things you would like to do, such as traveling to the Italian Lakes in Northern Italy or biking through the United States. Be specific when making your list; for instance, volunteering one day a week at the local hospital or fund raising for cancer research with Memorial Sloan Kettering. The more specific you are, the easier it will be to determine what it will cost when you begin budgeting for your golden years. If you find it difficult to determine what your goals are, start outlining how you would like to enjoy your retirement in a general way. Whatever your situation may be, make a list and after giving it considerable thought, start developing specific things you would like to be involved with when the time comes for you to retire.

Listing your assets and anticipated income is the next important step in determining how you will live, not within your dreams, but within your budget. It's easy to ascertain where your assets are and the income that is received from pensions, IRAs, interest, dividends, and nontraditional sources from information that is readily available if you have a PC and the use of online banking that I mentioned previously.

Of utmost importance when developing a budget is when to start collecting Social Security and how that decision will determine the amount of money that you will be receiving for the rest of your life. It would be nice to have saved enough to retire in comfort without considering Social Security benefits, but unfortunately most people must consider that income to make their retirement plans a reality and to have some degree of financial security. The longer people are able to wait to claim Social Security benefits, the greater the amount of their monthly checks for them and their families. Persons who claim benefits before their full retirement year are penalized by not receiving credits that are available to those who wait, and their payments are decreased accordingly. Good places to determine anticipated benefits are at www.aarp.com and accessing their "AARP's Social Security Benefits Calculator," and the Social Security website www.ssa.gov. The information will help in determining the best time to claim benefits that will coincide with your plans. It's always a good idea to consult a financial advisor to determine the most monetarily advantageous time to retire.

Retiring and collecting full benefits depends on a person's age. If you retire at full retirement age, you can work and earn as much as you want and keep all of your Social Security benefits. But, if you are younger than full retirement age when you retire, you may receive all of your benefits provided they don't exceed certain limits, as follows:

- The full retirement age increases gradually each year until it reaches age 67 for people born in 1960 or later.
- If you are at full retirement age or older in 2012, there is no limit on earnings.
- If you retire before full retirement age, for every $2 over the limit of $15,120, $1 is withheld from benefit payments.
- If you reach full retirement age in 2013, for every $3 over the limit of $40,080, $1 is withheld from benefits until the month you reach retirement age in that year.

Your full retirement age depends on the years in which you were born:

Born on or before 1937	65
1938	65 and 2 months
1939	65 and 4 months
1940	65 and 6 months
1941	65 and 8 months
1942	65 and 10 months
1943-1954	66
1955	66 and 2 months
1956	66 and 4 months
1957	66 and 6 months
1958	66 and 8 months
1959	66 and 10 months
1960	and later 67

A person can begin receiving benefits as early as age 62; however, the retirement benefits will be reduced by 5/9ths of 1 percent for every month between their effective date of retirement and their full retirement age, for up to 36 months, then the benefits will be reduced by 5/12ths of 1 percent thereafter. For example, if a person's full retirement age is 67, the individual will receive about 30% less when retiring at age 62. Conversely, if retirement is postponed past the full retirement age, benefits will increase. For example, depending on a person's age, each month a person delays retiring, a certain percentage will be added to their benefit payments until age 70. To be specific, if a person is born in 1936 and continues working past retirement age, benefits will increase 6% a year until retirement, ending at age 70. A person born in 1943 or later can increase benefits by 8% a year by working past full retirement age until age 70. In addition, working past full retirement will add years to Social Security earnings and may increase the benefit payments if earnings are higher than in prior years.

Many people do not want to retire at 62 or even at 67 years of age, but would rather continue working. As 60 is the new 50, many people are able to work 15 or even 20 years after full retirement, either on a full time or part time basis. If someone is inclined to continue working after receiving Social Security benefits, it's important to know how their supplemental income will affect and possibly reduce their Social Security payments. It's wise to consult with a financial professional before making any decisions that, once made, cannot be changed, and could prove to be costly for the rest of a person's life. One simple example of a costly mistake is choosing the wrong date to retire. If it's the later part of a year, it's possible that the $15,120 or $40,080 limits may have been exceeded and the recipient will be penalized by having benefit payments reduced accordingly.

Another important concern is what's considered as wages or earnings for Social Security purposes. The Administration defines "earned income" as "income from wages or net earnings from self-employment." For example, in addition to wages, earnings may include bonuses, commissions, and severance pay. What is not included are: investment income, pensions, capital gains, IRAs, and inheritances. Again, it's wise to consult with a financial advisor or the Social Security Administration before making decisions that will probably affect you adversely.

Another important consideration is that if you work past full retirement age without collecting benefits and do not have medical coverage at your place of employment, you can still enroll in Medicare.

The Initial Enrollment Period begins three months before your 65th birthday and ends three months after your 65th birthday.

There are two types of strategies that may be beneficial to retirees; they are "File and Suspend" and "Free Spousal Benefits." It's strongly suggested that before deciding to take advantage of either method that a financial professional should get involved with the decision making. Both strategies are complicated and, once made, may be difficult to change. A brief summary of these options can be found at the Social Security website: www.ssa.gov/retire2/suspend.htm. Following the instructions at the site can further explain the opportunities and disadvantages of these options. The Social Security Administration's summary at their website on this topic follows:

If you have reached full retirement age, but are not age 70, you can ask us to suspend retirement benefit payments as outlined below:

- **If you apply for benefits and we have not yet made a determination** that you are entitled, you may voluntarily suspend benefits for any month for which you have not received a payment. Your request to suspend benefits may include any retroactive benefits that might be due.
- **If you and your current spouse are full retirement age,** one of you can apply for retirement benefits now and have the payments suspended, while the other applies only for spouse's benefits. This strategy allows both of you to delay receiving retirement benefits on your own records so you can get delayed retirement credits. If you want to do this, only one of you can apply for retirement benefits and have the payments suspended.
- **If you are already entitled to benefits,** you may voluntarily suspend current or future retirement benefit payments up to age 70, beginning the month after the month when you made the request.

A special reminder to retirees: We pay Social Security benefits the month after they are due. If you contact us in June and request that we suspend benefits, you will still receive your June benefit payment in July.

- You do not have to sign documents to suspend benefit payments. You may ask us orally or in writing.
- If you started receiving Social Security benefits less than 12 months ago and you change your mind about when they start, you may be able to withdraw your Social Security claim and re-apply at a future date.

If your request is approved, you must repay all the benefits you and your family received based on your retirement application.

Before You Make Your Decision there are some things you need to know about what will happen if you suspend your retirement benefits:

- **If you are enrolled in Medicare Part B** (Supplementary Medical Insurance), **you will be billed** by the Centers for Medicare & Medicaid Services (CMS) **for future Part B premiums.** These premiums cannot be deducted from your suspended retirement benefits. If you do not pay the premiums timely, you may lose your Part B Medicare coverage. (You will have the option of automatically paying the bill from an account at your bank or financial institution).

There is an exception: if you also receive benefits as a spouse or ex-spouse, we can deduct your Part B premium from that benefit payment.

Our representatives can help you explore your options. Give us a call at **1-800-772-1213** or visit your local Social Security office.

As we can see from the above summary, the options can afford advantages, but do have exceptions, so again, hiring an expert consultant will pay in increased benefits that can add to your financial security.

As an example of how complicated and uncertain Social Security benefits may become, AARP sent out a newsletter that they requested be forwarded to everyone in the country. It's titled "Social Security Now Called Federal Benefit Payment/Entitlement!" It continues:

This isn't a benefit-It's earned income!

Not only did we all contribute to Social Security, but our employers did too.

It totaled 15% of our income before taxes.

If you averaged $30K per year over your working life, at 15% that's close to $180,000 invested in Social Security. If you calculate the future value of your monthly investment in the system ($375/month, including your employer's contribution) at a meager 1% interest rate compounded monthly, after 40 years of working you'd have over $1.3 million dollars saved! This is your personal investment. Upon retirement, if you took only 3% per year, you would receive $39,318 a year, or $3,277 a month.

That's almost three times more than today's average Social Security benefit of $1,230 per month according to Social Security Administration (Google it – it's a fact). And your retirement fund would last more than 33 years (until you're 98 if you retire at age 65)!

The full article can be read on AARP's website. The message the government seems to be sending is that they are going to make some drastic reductions in Social Security payments, either by reducing payments or making adjustments to the qualification requirements.

The current Co-Chair, Senator Alan Simpson, from the state of Wyoming is quoted as saying:

"That senior citizens are the Greediest Generation" as he compared Social Security to a "Milk Cow with 310 million teats."

Hopefully, there will be no major changes in our Social Security benefits, but with attitudes in the Senate such as Simpson's, who knows where, when, or how much it may costs us. This is another good reason to become a member of AARP as they are fighting against any reduction in Social Security payment and need all the support they can get in defending us against this unfair attitude that seems to be growing among our representatives in Congress.

A Lump Sum Windfall from Social Security

You can get a lump sum distribution if you delay benefits, but there are some disadvantages. If you are past full retirement age and are in need of money, a **Lump Sum** distribution may satisfy your financial needs. Little known Social Security options allow seniors to receive lump sum payments that can amount to thousands and in some cases tens of thousands of dollars.

To qualify for a lump sum payment, you must start receiving benefits after reaching full retirement age. You can find your full retirement age at ssa.gov/pubs/ageincrease.htm. At full retirement age, you are entitled to 100% of benefits. If you claim earlier, you will receive less; if you delay the amount you receive, as previously discussed, your benefits will increase roughly 8% more for each year you delay claiming them, until you reach age 70.

If you claim benefits after full retirement age, you can elect to receive a lump sum payment of up to six months' benefits. Consider a person who filed and suspended to age 69. He is in need of some quick money and decides to go for a lump sum distribution. If his full retirement age benefit was $2,000 a month, then the amount of his lump-sum distribution would be $72,000. The calculation takes him back to his receiving social security benefits at age 66 and therefore he has 36 months X $2,000 = $72,000 lump sum coming to him. I like the example that Robin Brewton of www.socialsecuritysolutions.com emailed me and I'm repeating below:

> An individual is assumed to be born on Jan. 2 for the simplicity of this calculation. He has a primary insurance amount (full retirement benefit) of $2,400 a month. That amount, if claimed at age 70, would grow

to about $3,178 with 48 months of delayed retirement credits. In this scenario, the consumer would have filed for benefits at full retirement of 66, but immediately suspended them and did not claim a benefit. Then, at age 70 or immediately before, he could request reinstatement of his benefits all the way back to his full retirement age of 66. He would receive:

48 months of suspension X 2,400 = $115,200.

The person's benefit amount would begin the following month at $2,400 per month, the amount he would have received at full retirement age. He would then forfeit any delayed retirement credits on the benefit amount.

An interesting spin on the lump sum distribution of $115,200 comes from an article that appeared in the Encore Section of the Wall Street Journal on March 9, 2014. I questioned the benefits of receiving a lump sum payment and received the following email response from Glenn Ruffenach, News Editor-The Wall Street Journal. Some of the same information as the above article appears, but he does explain the down-side very clearly for anyone contemplating a lump sum payment. He also explains very clearly the benefits of receiving a lump sum distribution after reaching full retirement:

Michael, thanks for the note. The number $115,200 comes from multiplying the person's Social Security benefits at age 66 ($2,400) by 48 months—the number of months he waited beyond his full retirement age to begin collecting Social Security.

So...in a sense, no one really "wins" or loses" here. The person ends up with (essentially) the same amount of money whether he begins collecting benefits at age 66 or at age 70—but the money "arrives" in a different "format." If he starts collecting benefits at age 66, his next 48 monthly payments will total $115,200; if he decides to ask for a lump sum at age 70, he receives the same $115,200. (And after that, his monthly payments will be $2,400—the payment he would have received if he had started claiming benefits at age 66.)

So why do this? Perhaps there is an emergency at age 70—and the person needs the cash. Or perhaps the person just learned (to use a dramatic example) that he's about to die—in which case, he could give the $115,200 to a family member. Of course these numbers don't take into account the cost-of-living increases.

Thanks for writing

Glenn Ruffenach

Another case as explained by William Meyer, Chief executive of SocialSecuritySolutions.com, is:

A woman is entitled to a $2,784 monthly benefit at age 68. By taking a lump sum, she can pocket $16,008. But her monthly benefits will fall to $2,668—the amount she would have received had she started taking her benefits six months earlier, at age 67½. (The $16,008 comes from multiplying the monthly benefit at age 67½ by six months.).

Kia Anderson, a spokeswoman for the Social Security Administrates, illustrates another probable scenario:

Say a retiree reached full retirement age in November 2012, but then waited to file an application for Social Security Benefits until November 2013. In this example, the retiree might be entitled to retroactive benefits—paid in a lump sum—beginning from May

20013, or six months before he or she finally filed for benefits. Because of the six-month limitation on this rule, the first six months of benefits would effectively be gone for a retiree in this situation. But, for those who need a large chunk of cash for an emergency or for those who are in bad health and don't expect to live long, the six months of benefits that are still available may be much appreciated.

Still, there is a major drawback to claiming retroactive benefits in a lump sum. It will reduce your ongoing monthly Social Security benefits for the rest of your life. That means that retirees should examine their circumstances before choosing this option.

It really depends on a person's individual situation as to whether they would like to file for retroactive retirement benefits.

As we can see, lump sum benefits can be advantageous to people and their heirs if they are in poor health and do not have a long life expectancy, or if they are in need of financial assistance.

There are a multitude of ways to approach lump sum Social Security benefits. I strongly suggest that a professional, such as William Meyer at www.socialsecuritysolutions.com, be contacted to determine what the most advantageous scenario might be.

As there are no free rides, lump sum distributions may be taxable. On the IRS question and answer website, a question asked and answered explains very clearly how the complicated tax structure affects payments:

Question:

I received social security benefits this year that were back benefits for prior years. Do I amend my tax returns for prior years? Are the back benefits paid in this year for past years taxable for this year?

Answer:

You cannot amend returns for prior years to reflect Social Security benefits received in a single lump sum in a single year. You must include the taxable part of a lump sum payment of benefits received in the current year (reported to you on Form SSA-1099) in your current year's income, even if the payment includes benefits for an earlier year.

However, there are two ways to determine the amount of income to include:

1--you can use your current year's income to figure the taxable part of the total benefits received in the current year, **OR**

2—you may make an election to figure the taxable part of a lump sum payment for an earlier year separately, using your income from the earlier year.

You can select the lump sum election method if it lowers the taxable portion of your benefits as follows:

1—under this method, you refigure the taxable part of all your benefits (including the lump-sum payment) for the earlier year using that year's income,

2—then you subtract any taxable benefits for the year that you previously reported.

3—the remainder is the taxable part of the lump-sum payment. Add it to the taxable part of your benefits for the current year.

4—there are worksheets in Publication 915, *Social Security and Equivalent Railroad Retirement Benefits*, to help you calculate the taxable portion using this method.

After using the Publication 915 worksheets in determining that your Social Security benefits are non-taxable or partially taxable, depending on your total income from all other sources, here is how, according to IRS, to calculate what part of your benefits you must pay taxes on:

Base Amounts
The following base amounts are used in figuring your taxable Social Security:

Filing Status	Base	Additional
Single	$25,000	$34,000
Head of household	$25,000	$34,000
Married Filing Jointly	$32,000	$44,000

A simple explanation of the tax consequences can be found in detail at www.ssa.gov/planners/taxes.htm as follows:

No one pays federal income tax on more than 85% of his or her Social Security benefits, based on the Internal Revenue Service's rules, if you:

o File a federal tax return as an "individual" and your *combined income** is:
1-between $25,000 and $34,000, you may have to pay income tax on up to 50% of your benefits.
2-more than $34,000, up to 85% of your benefits may be taxable.

o File a "joint return" and you and your spouse have a *combined income** that is:
1-between $32,000 and $44,000, you may have to pay income tax on up to 50% of your benefits.
2-more than $44,000, up to 85% of your benefits may be taxable.

o Are married and file a "separate tax return," you probably will pay full taxes on your benefits.

*Your adjusted gross income, plus Nontaxable interest, plus ½ of your Social Security benefits = Your *"combined income"*

As we can see, determining the most advantageous type of lump sum benefit and paying the least possible taxes requires the guidance of a qualified Social Security professional. Not to consult with one could be a costly mistake, resulting in reduced Social Security benefits after a lump sum distribution and possibly paying unnecessary taxes.

Conservative Investments

One of the first things we learn in life is that our decisions, good or bad, stay with us for a long time. Poor decisions not only seem to stick around forever, but seem to be difficult to overcome once made. As odd as it may seem, most people decide to retire based on their age, which is a poor decision, when they should really decide the time is right based on how much money they have and the ability of their assets to support them comfortably through their retirement, which could be 10, 20, or even 30 years. Retirement is about independence, not age, and money is what determines the amount of independence a person will have. Now here comes the tricky part. When should people start to switch their saving and investments to conservative income producing ones? And what options do they have? We all know that risk is an integral part of investing. When we were in our 30s and 40s, we could afford to take greater risks in the hope of receiving greater returns. If we lost money, we had decades to try to recover. But when we approach our 50s and 60s, we need to aggressively shift out of potentially volatile investments and into more conservative income producing ones. Large losses during retirement can be devastating to our pockets and stressful to our health at a point in time when we do not have the stamina or quickness of mind to sustain such unwelcomed events. Consider the arithmetic of a major loss. Let's say you have a $1 million dollar portfolio and lose 50% percent of it, reducing your holdings to half that amount. If you subsequently regain 50%, your portfolio value will be worth $750,000. To become whole would require a 100% percent increase; therefore, the greater the loss, the more difficult it will become to get back to where you started.

The 2008-2009 market crash caught many people that were

planning retirement "flat footed." Many of the 78 million boomers approaching retirement got caught up in the **"make a quick buck in the stock market"** frenzy, along with everyone else that didn't learn from the 2000-2003 stock market crash. Most of their stock holdings were in growth securities instead of more conservative investments, resulting in many investors having to postpone their retirement plans and continue working. It's easy, in hindsight, to discuss how people should have conducted themselves financially before a crisis. But what steps should people take and where should they place their funds when preparing for retirement? I can only discuss how we planned for our retirement and sustained only minor reductions in our portfolios during the aforementioned stock market crashes.

Being a Certified Public Accountant set the stage for my being a little more conservative than most. Till age 50, most of my investments were in aggressive blue chip stocks that paid dividends. I very rarely invested in stocks unless they had a history of paying dividends consistently. After age 50, I used a formula that I developed through my dealings in the financial community, and that is to invest your age in quality bonds, including municipal bonds and the balance in conservative dividend-paying blue chip stocks. So, at age 50, my portfolio included that percentage of bonds and 50% in dividend-paying conservative blue chip stocks. As time progressed, my holdings in bonds continued to match my age, but when I reach age 60, I decided to invest almost all of my portfolios in bonds and U.S. Treasuries, as my retirement time was nearing and I was more concerned about a safe income flow than asset growth.

Sounds good? Well, not so good; my 401K plan, our IRAs and our brokerage accounts that were heavily invested in bonds have had their ups and downs like everyone else, but we stayed our course without panicking and were fortunate enough to reach retirement with a good degree of financial security. You might ask what bonds we decided to invest in. Many years ago, I fell in love with the income flow from tax-free Closed End Municipal Bond Funds for my regular investment portfolio and blue chip corporate debt for our IRAs and my 401K plan. In addition to what I thought were relatively safe investments, the income from the municipal bonds were tax free and the interest from the corporate debt that accrued in our retirement accounts was not taxed until we began our Required Minimum Distributions (RMD) at 70½ years of age. My plan may seem too good to be true, so a brief rundown of what these types of investments are about is in order:

> **Closed End Municipal Bond Funds**—Municipal bonds, also called munis, are bonds issued by a state, city, or other local governments, and are traded on the three major stock exchanges, just like regular stocks. Issuers usually include states, cities, counties, redevelopment agencies, school districts, and any other government entity within a state that is authorized to borrow money in that fashion. Municipal bonds may be general obligations bonds, which are backed by the full faith of the issuer, but are generally secured by specified revenues, such as sales tax, or they may be bonds for specific projects within the states, such as construction of bridges and tunnels. Interest income received by the holders of the bonds is often exempt from federal income tax and from the income tax of the state in which it is issued if the holder is a resident of that state. The bonds usually pay interest semi-annually until maturity, then the face amount of the bond is paid to the holder. A taxable equivalent of a bond yielding 5% for someone in the 31% tax bracket is 7.2% and higher if the bond is for the state that the holder is domiciled. Tax-free munis pay an interest rate higher than T-Notes and T-Bills because they are considered to have a greater risk of failure. While unusual, it's possible for the issuer to go broke and declare bankruptcy. To reduce that risk, many investors buy municipal bond funds that pool together portfolios of bonds from different sources within a state or by combining munis from different states into a national fund. Many funds can have 20 or more different bonds in their portfolios, which satisfies many investors who

like diversification and safety all wrapped up into one neat package. Some funds are actually insured as to principal, but since the 2008 crash, many of the main insurers, such as AIG Insurance Company, who almost went bankrupt trying to cover many of their insured banks investment losses, have become very selective in what financial securities they will insure.

Closed-end funds issue a set number of shares that trade on the stock exchanges like any other security, and are subject to fluctuations from the net asset value (NAV) of the bonds within the fund, resulting in the funds selling at a discount or premium. Most funds pay interest or dividends monthly, which can be reinvested at the market price without a commission or the money can be sent directly to checking accounts for instant use. When the fund is selling at a discount and income is reinvested, the new shares are purchased at the discounted price, which increases the return on investments; conversely, when they are purchased at a premium, the rate of return on the purchased shares decreases.

One of the reasons I was attracted to this type of investment was the safety in the diversification that pooling of many government bonds offered. Another great feature is the ability to automatically reinvest income, at no charge. If the income is needed, it can be deposited into your account of choice, whether it be a savings, brokerage, or checking account. In the 15-plus years that I have been involved with these funds, there has never been a missed or late payment. Currently, the yield on many of my funds is between 5% to 7% tax free, which is a hell of a lot more than banks are paying, and in my opinion a lot safer, considering that currently there are some major banks that might be forced into bankruptcy or receivership. An important note is that the income from municipal bonds is not subject to the new 3.8% Federal and possibly state "Tax on Unearned Investment Income," which makes these securities all the more attractive as the effective rate of return is increased accordingly.

There are many places to research Closed End Funds; my favorite is www.morningstar.com. To show how readily available information is, a copy of one of my positions that is listed with Morningstar and just one of the many pages that includes investment data follows:

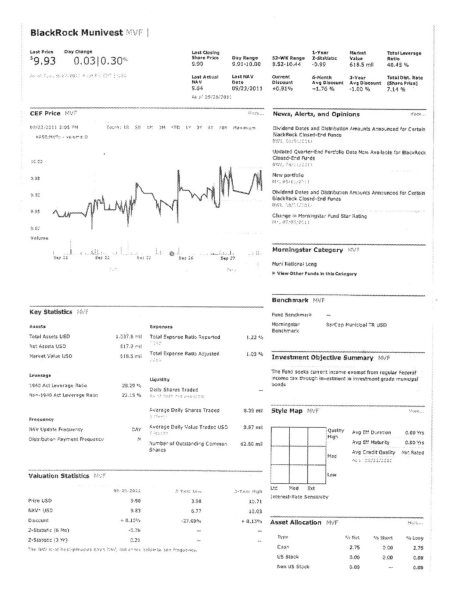

Morningstar also has a "Watch List" available where an investor's stocks and bonds can be listed and followed on a daily basis, which is a useful method of keeping track of price fluctuations and any current news on the holdings that are listed. It also has readily available information if Morningstar changes its star ratings for securities listed on your Watch List or if there is important news information about a given security on the list.

There are three instances when I choose to sell my closed end munis:

- When the market value of a fund increases 15% over my purchase price. At that time I will sell my position and replace it with a different closed end muni fund. The new purchase may also be in the same category as the previous one, such as selling a Nuveen fund and replacing it with a different Nuveen fund. There is no tax penalty as it is not considered a short sale. Of course, I will recognize a capital gain on the transaction, and pay taxes at regular capital gain rates for Federal and State taxes.
- If I have capital gains that I want to offset to reduce my taxes, I might sell positions that have capital losses. This, in effect, reduces my tax liabilities and also helps me realign my closed end funds into more attractive positions paying more interest or into a fund with a higher Morningstar rating.
- Being that much of my muni funds' interest is reinvested, there are times that I will withdraw funds that are necessary to supplement my income.

The following is a review of the main advantages of tax free Municipal Bond Funds for senior citizens:

- **Potential Safety of Income**—On March 7, 2012, Moody's Investor Service published research that stated that investment grade municipal bonds had an average cumulative default rate of just 0.08% between 1970 and 2011. This shows that there is some risk of principal loss in muni investments. But if funds are purchased having a mixture of bonds from different sources, the risk of loss should be diminished accordingly.
- **Potential for Predictable Income**—Closed End Funds pay dividends monthly and can be relied upon when predicting a

person's income flow in the preparation of a budget that is so necessary when contemplating retirement.

- **Potential Triple Tax-Free Income**—income from muni funds is not subject to federal income tax and—depending on where your permanent home is—may not be subject to state and city taxes as well. As I mentioned previously, I've been investing in these closed end funds for over 15 years and have never had a missed payment.

- **Corporate Debt**—I'm not suggesting that buying corporate bonds is for everyone; I'm just reflecting the kind of securities that made me feel comfortable while returning attractive interest income into my retirement accounts. The bonds that I have invested in are called **Exchange-Traded Debt Securities** and are traded on the stock exchanges rather than in the bond markets. The securities include debentures, notes, and bonds and resemble preferred stocks in their basic features. In liquidation, they rank junior to a company's secured debt, are equal to other unsecured debt, and are senior to a company's preferred and common stocks. These debts are generally issued in $25 denominations and can be short term or could have maturity dates of 30 years or more. A nice feature is that the securities are normally redeemable at the issuer's option, on or after five years from the date of issue at par value. I have been pleasantly surprised on many occasions when this has happened to me, especially when I purchased the positions at a discount, which I usually do. When this happens, I receive a nice profit in addition to the interest that I had already received for many years. The gains from the calls were not immediately taxed as they were holdings in our IRAs and my 401K plan and were tax deferred until we withdrew the funds. Most of the debt securities pay quarterly interest distributions. Some of the corporations listed are AT&T Inc., Comcast Corp., Ford Motors Credit, MetLife Inc., Sears Roebuck Acceptance, and my favorite, General Electric Capital. The above corporations pay from 5% to 7% annually, and if the securities are in IRAs or other pension plans, the interest accumulates tax free until distributions are taken. As can be seen by the corporations listed, the bonds are primarily backed by each company's reputation as a leader in the financial community. A useful website to research these securities is www.quantumonline.com. A description of one of my holdings listed with Quantum's Online financial information follows:

by Ticker Symbol

Search

Welcome Back, Michael Bivona

Home   Income Tables   Income Lists   Stock Lists   Special Lists   Services   Information   Login

General Electric Capital Corp., 6.625% Public Income Notes PINES due 6/28/2032
Ticker Symbol: GEA   CUSIP: 369622527   Exchange: NYSE
Security Type: Exchange-Traded Debt Security

QUANTUMONLINE.COM SECURITY DESCRIPTION: General Electric Capital Corp., 6.625% Public Income NotES (PINES), issued in $25 denominations, redeemable at the issuer's option on or after 6/28/2007 at $25 per share plus accrued and unpaid interest, maturing 6/28/2032, distributions of 6.625% ($1.65625) per annum are paid quarterly on 3/28, 6/28, 9/28 & 12/28 to holders of record one business day prior to the payment date while the securities remain in global security form (note that the ex-dividend date is at least 2 business days prior to the record date). Distributions paid by these debt securities are interest and as such are NOT eligible for the 15% tax rate on dividends and is also NOT eligible for the dividend received deduction for corporate holders. Units are expected to trade flat, which means accrued interest will be reflected in the trading price and the purchasers will not pay and the sellers will not receive any accrued and unpaid interest. The PINES are senior, unsecured obligations of the company and will rank equally with all existing and future unsecured and unsubordinated indebtedness of the company. See the IPO prospectus for further information on the debt securities by clicking on the 'Link to IPO Prospectus' provided below.

Stock Exchange	Cpn Rate Ann Amt	LiqPref CallPrice	Call Date Matur Date	Moodys/S&P Dated	Distribution Dates	15% Tax Rate
NYSE Chart	6.63% $1.65625	$25.00 $25.00	6/28/2007 6/28/2032	Aa3 / AA+ 8/27/11	3/28, 6/28, 9/28 & 12/28 Click for MW ExDiv Date Click for Yahoo ExDiv Date	No

Goto Parent Company's Record (GE)

IPO - 8/20/2002 - 40.00 Million Notes @ $25.00/note.   Link to IPO Prospectus
Market Value $ 1 Billion
Click for current GEA price quote from the NYSE

Company's Online Information Links
HOME PAGE: http://www.ge.com/
Company's Investor Relations Information   Goto Investor Relations Information
Company's Online News Releases   Goto News Releases
Online Company Profile   Goto Online Profile

Company's Online SEC EDGAR Filings
Company's SEC EDGAR Filings   Goto SEC Filings

Company's Email Address Links
Email Address   ir.contacts@corporate.ge.com

Unfortunately, although the above security had a maturity date of 2032, it was called as I was writing this section, but GE issued two other positions, GEB and GEH, both paying 4.875%, which I purchased as soon as the positions became available. The interest on both of these positions is still a lot higher than the current average bank interest of 1% or less and will accumulate in our IRAs, interest-deferred, until our required annual mandatory distributions must be made. The IRA distributions are subject to a taxpayer's regular tax rates for Federal and State income taxes, but are not subject to the new 3.8% Medicare Tax on Unearned Investment Income.

Excerpts from an article written by James A. Klotz, President of FMS Bonds, Inc., dated 2/24/2014, sums up how important tax free municipal bonds are in light of the recent tax increases, especially for seniors. Taxes went up, not only for the highest earners, but also for people with more modest means:

Uncle Sam wants more

Have you slogged through your taxes yet?

If so, you understand just how dramatically the landscape has changed. If not, brace yourself: hikes, as noted by CNNMoney, can be attributed to last year's Congressional deal to avoid the "fiscal cliff" as well as provisions in the Affordable Care Act.

For the highest earners, the top income-tax rate was boosted from 35% to 39.6%, with tax rates on dividends and long-term capital gains going to 20% from 15%.

There is also a new 3.8% Medicare tax on net investment income that affects some or all of taxable capitals gains, dividends, interest, rental income, and annuities.

Higher taxes and you

What does this mean for your investments?

Let's say you're a California resident. According to figures by Bloomberg, if you're among the highest earners—that is, you're paying the highest federal and state income-tax rates, plus the 3.8% Medicare surcharge—your combined tax rate would be 50.83%. In New York, it would be 48.73%, and 45.25% if you're a Pennsylvania resident.

For income investors seeking attractive rates, those eye-popping tax rates will require stratospheric pre-tax yields.

When the tax increases were originally discussed, the full impact of Uncle Sam's elevated appetite did not immediately register with the majority of investors. Now that the tax ramifications have hit home, interest in the Muni Market has surged. Fact is, no other financial instrument offers a similar level of security and return. Consequently, munis have outperformed other fixed-income markets recently.

High quality long-term munis are currently yielding between 4.5% and 5.00%. To equal that 4.5% return, investors would need taxable equivalents in the states listed below of:

STATES	HIGHEST TAX RATES	TAX EQUIVALENT FOR 4.5% TAX-FREE YIELD
CA	50.83%	9.10%
FL	43.40%	7.95%
HI	50.04%	9.00%
MA	46.57%	8.40%
NJ	48.82%	8.80%
NY	48.73%	8.78%

As we can see, municipal bonds are certainly a nice safe investment paying exciting tax-free income. If Closed End Municipal Bond Funds are purchased, not only are the tax-free returns somewhat higher, but the numerous bonds within the funds makes investments safer, as it provides the magic word for retirees, **diversification**. Before investing in these funds, check with www.morningstar.com for important financial information, including how many stars Morningstar researchers have given to each listed fund in their wide range of choices.

Preparing for retirement is about accumulating wealth through savings and investment performance. But in retirement, our primary goal becomes more complex, and continuing growth without depleting the core of our holdings becomes our objective, if possible. Making sure that we have a steady stream of income to cover our lifestyle without tapping into principal is paramount to a financially successful retirement. To help accomplish this, hiring an experienced financial advisor is imperative to assist with retirement financial planning; not to do so could result in a major financial catastrophe and might mean the difference between retirement bliss or retirement grief.

Deadly Investment Sins

Whether you are a seasoned investor or a casual one, all investors make mistakes with their choice of investments. The important thing is to minimize them by taking tried and true measures that will reduce the possibility of making costly errors.

As we all know, when you lose money, someone else is gaining by your misfortune. This makes investing attractive to scammers or organizations that take creative liberties with their financial information to make their shares attractive to investors. A popular method for investment scammers is through the use of emails, which, according to the Federal Trade Commission site, www.onguardonline.gov, is listed in the top 10 email scams.

Considering that the markets shift unpredictably and that trying to get accurate financial information can be very time consuming, confusing, and in many cases elusive, it's wise at every level to have a professional financial advisor at your side before entrusting your hard earned funds to strangers. This is especially true when dealing with salesmen whose livelihood depends on your investing with them. I could never understand why salesmen are allowed to solicit and advise investors about their finances when they, in effect, make a commission on money invested from their suggestions. Strangely, they get their commission whether or not the investment advice is successful.

In my case, I found that following seven cardinal rules have kept me out of harm's way. I'm not claiming that every investment I ever made was wise or successful, but following certain disciplines is as good a way as any to limit financial losses in the stock market.

- **Always Have a Plan**—an investment plan should drive all of your investment decisions. Without a sound plan, which should be discussed with a professional financial advisor and reviewed periodically, you may make decisions that are ill-suited to your goals. A proper plan should include disciplines and satisfy your objectives. A professional financial advisor that you trust can help you develop a plan that supports your expectations, while considering your preferences and tolerance for risk and volatility. Remember: your retirement plan should be income based with protection of principal, if possible.

- **Diversify**—putting most of your eggs in one basket is not only unwise, but can also be dangerous as it could cost you to lose most of your investments if there is a major decline in the stock market or in your individual holdings. Keep in mind that even reputable organizations and industries can get into financial trouble, resulting in their stocks tumbling.

- **Don't Bite off More Than You Can Chew**—don't take diversification too far by buying every stock that you think will make you money and causing your portfolio to become difficult to manage. Diversify, but do so wisely while staying within the parameter of your investment plan.

- **Emotions = Lust**—don't invest your hard earned money in stocks based on hearsay of friends or the news media's hype.

If the tip sounds too good to be true, it probably is too good to be true. Also, don't fall in love with a stock or industry; remember, "They can't love you back." Many poor financial decisions are made because of invalid performance expectations. Always let the historical facts drive your conclusions instead.

- **Reacting to Current Events**—investing because of market swings or current trends can be costly mistakes and may not pay off in the long run. Likewise, trying to time the market or making decisions based on current activity or what's read in the news media can also put a dent in your retirement funds. Only invest after proper research and stay within your retirement plan.

- **Don't be Impatient**—remember, retirement plans are for the long haul. The markets fluctuate daily, weekly, and annually, but the trend over long periods of time has always been up. Patience pays off, so don't churn your wisely researched positions by selling on a whim or to make a killing or by "playing the markets." Investing is not a game, so don't play at it.

- **Chasing Returns Without Considering the Risks**—remember Bernard Madoff? Of course you do, so you won't be surprised when I say not to expect exorbitant annual returns on your investments. Investing in imaginary sure things in the hope of gaining better-than-average returns can be risky, foolish, and without a doubt, greedy. Avoid get-rich-quick promises. If salespeople, such as the likes of Madoff, try to convince you that they are doing you a favor if you invest with them, run at full speed from their presence. A popular scheme of the "master salesman" Madoff was to be secretive about how he earned better-than-average returns for his investors. He actually convinced people that they couldn't understand the complicated financial maneuvering he used to reward his flock with high returns for over 20 years. So his victims were content with receiving high annual returns on their investments without inquiring as to the method or source of their income. **So, do not ever invest in anything that you do**

not fully understand. Once your retirement plan is in place, stick with it and you'll be surprised at how it will sustain you in your retirement. Again, a professional financial advisor should be consulted periodically to make sure that your investment decisions are in accordance with your retirement objectives.

While we are on the subject of Bernard Madoff, I think it's a good opportunity to discuss exactly what he did to steal approximately 65 billion dollars from religious and charitable organizations, pension plans, celebrities, and little old ladies. Oddly enough, he targeted Jewish organizations and people, mostly those belonging to country clubs in Long Island, New York, and Palm Beach, Florida. As you can see from the locations, both places are where Barbara and I spend our time in retirement. Needless to say, I'm familiar with people who thought their 10 to 12 percent returns were a sure thing, even though most of their friends were receiving modest returns on their investments. Their underlying trust was the fact that he himself was Jewish, so they invested blindly and enjoyed their high returns on paper, no questions asked. The ones that suffered the greatest losses were those who didn't receive cash payments of the high yields but reinvested their money in anticipation of receiving even higher returns. In this group were religious and charitable organizations that parked their investments and watched its spectacular growth, on paper, over the years. They became, if you will, participants in building not a "house of cards" but a "skyscraper of cards," due to the fact that they were content with letting their money accumulate for long periods of time without investigating why they were receiving such unusually high returns, especially during poor financial periods. As much has been written about Madoff, I think Wikipedia summarized the financial fiasco pretty well:

> Madoff's operation differed from a typical Ponzi scheme. While most Ponzis are based on nonexistent businesses, Madoff's brokerage operation was very real. Madoff was a "master marketer." His fund was considered exclusive, giving the appearance of a

"velvet rope." He generally refused to meet directly with investors, which gave him an "OZ" aura and increased the allure of the investments. Some Madoff investors were wary of removing their money from his fund, fearing that they could not get back in later.

Madoff's annual returns were unusually consistent, around 10%, and were a key factor in perpetuating the fraud. Ponzi schemes typically pay returns of 20% or higher, and collapse quickly. Some authorities believe that he started his deception in the 1970s.

Mitchell Zuckoff, professor of journalism at Boston University and the author of *Ponzi's Scheme: The True Story of a Financial Legend*, says, "The 5% payout rule," a federal law requiring private foundations to pay out 5% of their funds each year, allowed Madoff's Ponzi scheme to go undetected for a long period of time since he managed money mainly for charities. He notes, "For every billion dollars in foundation investment, Madoff was effectively on the hook for about $50 million in withdrawals a year. If he was not making real investments, at that rate the principal would last for 20 years if there were no new investors to feed the pot of gold. By targeting charities, he could avoid the threat of sudden unexpected withdrawals."

In his guilty plea, Madoff admitted that he hadn't actually traded since the early 1990s, and all of his returns since then had been fabricated.

With the general market collapse of 2008, investors, including charities, started withdrawing their money from Madoff's funds. Of course, it wasn't long before he ran out of cash, which caused his empire to come tumbling down, with a purported loss of approximately 65 billion dollars in assets. Even investors like Stephen Spielberg and Keven Bacon, who I'm sure had financial consultants, lost most of their invested money with him.

To show how even sophisticated investors get taken, the following is a list of some of the investors who, as reported by The Wall Street Journal in their March 24, 2014 issue, got "skinned" by Madoff's Ponzi scheme:

- **Fairfield Greenwich Advisors**, an investment management firm, exposed half of their 14 billion dollars of their investors' assets, or 7 billion dollars, with Madoff's phantom companies.
- **Kingate Management**, a hedge fund with 2.8 billion in investors' assets, invested heavily with Madoff.
- **HSBC**, a British bank that invested their institutional clients' funds with Madoff and put a billion dollars of their investors funds at risk.
- **Bank Medici**, an Austrian bank invested over 2 billion dollars of their investors' funds with the Madoff organization.

The above organizations were considered safe places to deposit or invest funds because they were in the financial business and considered knowledgeable when it came to finances. How unfortunate their investors were when their hard earned money was put at risk.

They were not the only ones that should have known better and were duped. Madoff's favorite clients were nonprofit organizations who are required by law to account for their financial activities to the Treasury Department, as they have a strict fiduciary responsibility, and their investments should be on the conservative side. Some of the popular nonprofits that evidentially didn't adhere to wise conservative investment guidelines that were also listed in the same Wall Street Journal article were:

- **The Jewish Community Foundation of Los Angeles**, which is the largest manager of charitable gift assets for Los Angeles Jewish philanthropists, invested 18 million dollars of their clients' funds with Madoff's phantom organization.
- **North Shore-Long Island Jewish Health System** invested over 5 million dollars with the Madoff organization. A donor volunteered to reimburse the Jewish Health System for any losses that they will incur.

- **Hadassah**, a women's Zionist organization, invested over 90 million dollars with Madoff, and was confident that a person of Jewish heritage would invest their money honestly and wisely.
- **International Olympic Committee** was the Olympic organizer that put almost 5 million dollars at risk by investing with Madoff.

It's interesting to note that some popular celebrities were also on the same list. They either didn't have qualified financial advisors or their advisors didn't do their homework when it came to protecting their clients' money, by practicing conservative financial strategies. Some familiar names are:

- **Kevin Bacon and wife Kyra Sedgwick**, who are Hollywood actors and invested with the "slick one" but would not divulge how much money they had at risk.
- **Zsa Zsa Gabor**, who needs no introduction. The actress's lawyer stated that the actress, who was 91 years old at the time of the crash, may have lost 10 million dollars.
- **Sandy Koufax**, the former outstanding Los Angeles Dodger pitcher, invested heavily with the "crook-of-two-centuries," but no amount was available.
- **Larry King,** the talk show host, also invested heavily with the manipulator, but no amount was available in The Wall Street Journal's article.

What more can be said? Greed is blinding when it comes to investing in the stock market. If an investment seems **too good to be true,** step back and take a good look at the history of the organization, and consult with a qualified investment advisor, one who does not get a commission on your investments, but charges only for services rendered. Together, you and your advisor should make rational decisions in accordance with your retirement plans that will result in a fulfilling financially secured retirement, with a reduced risk of losing hard earned money.

Unnecessary Risks Investors Take

Stock Risks—this is when stocks that you own go down the tubes, like Enron and Global Crossing. Choose the wrong stock and you're at great risk; choose the right stock and you can realize great profits. If you want to make the most money, invest in one stock. If you want to lose the most money, invest in one stock. The most conservative solution for retirees and soon-to-be-retirees is to own hundreds of stocks, and this is accomplished by owning well established mutual funds, which results in having a diverse portfolio. This provides a safety net and should always be foremost in your strategy when planning for retirement income and protection of assets.

Industry Risks—this carries the same risk as owning one stock. Putting all or most of your money into stocks in only one industry can result in wiping out your portfolio in a down market. Some people think that it's safe because they are familiar with the industry or the media hypes the industry as the trend of the future. I know many people that fell in love with technology companies that peaked in the early in 2000s in a wave of optimism. Many stuffed their pension plans with technology stock and for a while thought they would be able to retire comfortable due to the increase in the asset value of their pension funds. They were shocked after the crash; many had to postpone their retirement plans because of the decrease in value of their investments in technology securities. Some folks with the same preferences who were already retired had to return to the labor market to sustain their lifestyle. The solution to this risk, again, is to diversify. If you're an industry investor, there are many mutual funds that have various industries in their portfolios. You'll have ownership in General Electric, Google, and even Berkshire Hathaway, so an occasional Global Crossing won't sink your retirement funds or your plans for the future.

Commissions and other Fee Risks—by paying high sales commissions and fees, you may be paying more than you need to for your investments, thereby increasing your cost and decreasing your potential profits. An example is if you invest $20,000 and pay a 5% commission, you immediately lose $1,000 increasing the amount that you must earn to break even. So it's imperative to ask in advance how much these charges are when buying securities. Keep in mind that it's not very difficult to trade yourself if you have access to a computer. I trade with Citibank and other firms and pay less than $20 per transaction, which doesn't put much of a dent in the cost of my portfolios.

It's also important to know what fees are paid after you purchase securities or mutual funds. It's imperative to research how much your annual costs will be within a fund, as high fees can result in a major dip in your portfolio. Expense information is sometimes hidden between the multitude of information that funds provide, including pension funds. As a matter of fact, as I'm writing this in February of 2014, the Department of Labor is trying to mandate additional guides to help "navigate disclosures about fees and potential conflicts of interest within pension plans." The proposed plan can be viewed in its entirety on the Department of Labor's website at www.dol.gov/find/20140311/.

A good place to find mutual fund and stock expense ratios is on Morningstar's website at www.morningstar.com. There is a copy and an appropriate example of one of their researched mutual fund's listing, including their expense ratio, in my Conservative Investments topic. So, as we can see, it's not only important to know exactly what the fees are when purchasing securities and mutual funds, but it's just as important to research what the cost of managing positions in your portfolio are, as they could reduce the value of your holdings substantially.

Tax Risks—no one wants to pay unnecessary taxes on their investments. So, as I previously mentioned, it's wise to put interest and dividend paying securities in deferred tax accounts, such as IRAs, 401Ks, and employer pension plans. The income and profits from investments will accumulate tax-deferred until withdrawn, in accordance with the required mandatory distribution rules, starting at age 70½. As previously mentioned, I was comfortable with purchases of General Electric debt securities in our IRAs and have seen the high interest yields multiply nicely, as no tax was paid on the income until we withdrew our mandatory funds. Mandatory withdrawal calculations are done by banks and brokerage companies for their customers, which is a really a nice feature, as they provide the amounts required to be withdrawn annually based on the balance in a person's account as of 12/31 of the prior year. They also notify the owner well in advance what the RMD is for the current year.

If you're inclined to invest in the stock market, my favorite conservative investments are closed end municipal bond funds, as previous discussed. The interest and dividends accumulate free of federal income tax and if the underlying bonds are from the city and state that you reside, they are also tax free for those taxes. A bonus is that reinvested income is not subject to commissions or other reinvestment charges.

Again, with the assistance of a qualified investment advisor, unnecessary risks can be reduced resulting in minimal reductions in investment values and a maximum reduction in personal stress.

Reducing Debt

Getting rid of debt before retiring makes budgeting a lot easier and certainly reduces stress that retirees do not need in their golden years. An example of how dangerous debt can be during retirement is illustrated by using a $500-a-month car payment. The payment is fixed while the income to pay for it may not be. If income is from interest or dividends, then any reduction in their rate of return can cause the debt to possibly go unpaid or to be paid out of principal, which in turn can be the beginning of the depletion of assets that are the basis of the income that is necessary for financial security during retirement. Many people pay off most of their debts before retiring, even if it means remaining in the workforce longer than planned. We all have experienced the interest rates in our savings accounts going below one percent, while many of us have been affected by public corporations reducing or eliminating their dividends. The two lessons that we should learn are to stay as debt free as possible prior to retirement, and not to rely on the stability of bank interest or dividend payments when developing a budget. Social Security benefits, annuities, reliable bond interest, and Treasuries are much more stable choices, unless you plan on using principal to supplement other revenue.

Unforeseen Expenses

Few of us head into retirement expecting bad things to happen with our finances. But bad, unforeseen things invariably do happen. In our case, we were lucky to learn from a bitter experience of friends. They were snowbirds and during a winter storm in New York, their pipes burst due to the failure of their heating system. They had oil-hot-water-baseboard heat with a computerized oil replenishment system. The system failed and the replacement of the precious oil never happened. To make a long story short, the basement flooded and the leaks from the upper pipes just about destroyed everything in their house. To make matters worse, this happened when they were spending quality time in Florida, far away from the cold wintery New York weather, and caused them to return to their home under the worst possible circumstances, in freezing weather no less. It took two years of living in hotels before the house was restored and their furnishings replaced. Their story sent us into a panic; we have the same type of heating system, baseboard hot water, except our furnace is gas operated. Even so, the possibility of broken pipes haunted me until I researched the subject to determine how I could overcome such an event.

The crux of the problem boils down to getting things done prior to retirement, when you have the energy and money is usually more readily available. We were already retired when we began our preventive maintenance journey, fortunately, before we had a disaster. First, we decided that our hot water gas furnace was getting on in years, so we replaced it and the hot water heater at the same time. Next, we had to figure out how we could shut off the water coming into our house when we were away for the winter months. We had friends that lived in upstate New York's Snowbelt that simply turned off their water when they left their homes for extended periods of time. Most have hot air heat, which reduces the number of pipes at risk of bursting, but I was intrigued with the possibility of turning off the water coming into my house, which kept me digging for an answer to alleviate the possibility of our having a similar disaster as our friends had experienced. Our plumber supplied us with the perfect solution. The first thing we had to do before turning off the supply of water coming into our home was to winterize the hot water baseboard heating system with antifreeze, just like it's done in automobiles. So if the heating pipes burst for some reason, the worst-case scenario would be 15 gallons of antifreeze leaking into the house instead of an ocean of water from our incoming fresh water system. The next thing we did was install an accustat; this is an electronic device that notifies us in Florida via land-line telephone with a backup radio phone that we installed in our attic, if the temperature in our house drops below 50 degrees. If it does, we immediately call our house sitter to investigate. Then the final and most important steps were: we turned off the water to the house and set the heating thermostat to 60 degrees and our hot water heater to vacation. The antifreeze that was put into the hot water heating system circulates and is self-contained, the same as in a car engine, and keeps the house above freezing, which gives us an amazing degree of comfort when we're away from our New York home in the freezing-snowy months, as we had this year of 2014.

At of this writing, February, 2014, my town in Long Island has had the worst weather in its history, and it didn't seem that the bad weather was ending. Last week, on a day that they got eight inches of snow, the ice and wind caused trees to fall and the roads to turn into ice. The inclement weather caused a two-hour power failure that shorted out one of the circulators that provided heat to the main level of our house. The temperature dropped to 40 degrees and activated the heat sensor. As designed, the sensor automatically dialed our answering service, who in turn called us. We called our house sitter and advised her of the heating problem. She couldn't respond because of the icy roads. We weren't worried about freezing pipes as the baseboard heat that we have was filled with antifreeze. The following day, our friend and house sitter Debby came to our house and called the service company, Home Service. They responded and replaced the circulator, which restored the heat to the main level of our home.

The story had a happy ending, but the point is that we had to spend thousands of dollars during our retirement that we hadn't planned on, which was not a happy ending. It put a considerable dent in our retirement funds, especially, being that our heating system was over

25 years old and we decided to replace it, which we should have done prior to retirement when our cash flow was stronger.

While we were on a preventive maintenance kick, we decided to replace our 25-year-old roof before leaks from it became a problem. While we were at it, we had several oak trees, which were over 80 feet high and a little too close to our house, removed and many others trimmed; luckily for us, two of the larger oak trees were infested with carpenter ants and were probably waiting for just the right inopportune time to fall on our house. If we'd been smart, we would have done all of the above before retiring, but being human, we waited for a **sign.** Fortunately, the **sign** was not our reality, but the reality of our dear friends when Hurricane Sandy hit Long Island and downed many of the large oak trees in our neighborhood, hitting many of the homes and causing incalculable damage to the structures and immeasurable damage to our friends' wellbeing. We had some large oak trees fall but fortunately they fell away from our home. These turned out to be major expenses that we hadn't considered prior to retiring, and put another considerable dent in our retirement funds.

So, if possible, it's wise to assess any likely future major expenses and to take care of them prior to retiring so that when budgeting funds for retirement, hopefully, most of the large possible expenses have already been paid.

Real Estate Tax Reductions

One of the highest burdens, if not the highest for homeowners, are the payment of real estate taxes that seem to increase annually for various politically motivated reasons. There are exemptions and reductions from the tax for any number of reasons, such as for people with disabilities, low income taxpayers, and for senior citizens. The amounts available depend on where you live and the consideration that the various towns, cities, and states give for the reduction of the taxes that swell governments' coffers.

I will discuss two reductions that I was lucky to qualify for that have reduced my expenses considerably; those are a reduction in my real estate taxes due to a **Grievance Filing** and a **Veterans Exemption.**

Grievance Filing

I'm embarrassed to say that I just received a reduction of over 20%, retroactive to the tax year the grievance was filed in 2011. In addition, we received a refund check for the same amount, as the reduction was approved by the taxing authorities in the 2012 tax year, which resulted in an overpayment of my prior year's taxes. Considering that we have been living in our New York residence for almost 40 years, I'm shocked that I didn't take advantage of the Grievance Filing previously, especially when I knew my neighbor had done so successfully a few years earlier. Oddly, he filed for another reduction after a two year waiting period, and received a second approval for a decrease that is yet to be determined.

So, senior citizens, don't waste any time researching if you're in a municipality that allows grievance filings, and if you are, I advise that you file the proper documents at your tax assessor's office or contact a real estate tax grievance consultant and turn you grievance over to their capable hands. After extensive research for a reputable consultant, we decided to use the same company, ZAPMYTAX, which was so successful with our neighbor's filings. Their website tells it all:

> Suffolk homeowners like you are feeling the pain of high property and school taxes. You may have filed for STAR (low income homeowners) or other exemption, but you may still be paying more than your fair share of taxes.
>
> A **Property Tax Grievance** is a formal complaint that is filed contesting a town's assessment value of a specific property. We can't change the calculations and rates the State and your town use to determine your Property Taxes. What we can challenge—and have reduced—is the taxable value of your home. If the Tax Assessor lowers that, the total taxes you pay are reduced because the assessment is lower.
>
> Many property owners worry that if they file a grievance, their taxes may be raised or someone from the assessor's office will come into their home.

We can assure you that neither of these things will happen. Upon filing the tax grievance, your property tax assessment can be lowered or remain the same, but cannot be increased and no one will come to your home (except our own assessor who reviews your property only from the outside). Rest assured that there will be:

- No risk of your Property Tax increasing due to a Grievance filing
- No inspections
- No reduction in your other exemptions, such as Stars (School Tax Relief) and Veterans exemption because of your filing
- No payment to us is due if we do not get a reduction in your Property Taxes (that is a pretty good incentive for us to 'get the job done.')
- No fee after first year's saving

Our Fees

When you give us authorization to file a Tax Grievance on your behalf, we handle the entire process for you. If we are successful in obtaining a Tax reduction for you, our fee is 50% of your first year's savings. **The savings you reap in subsequent years are entirely your own.** Here's an example of how it works:

Your taxes are calculated by multiplying your assessment by your tax rate. For example, if your taxes are $10,000 and we get it reduced to $8,000, your savings is $2,000 and our fee is 50% of the savings, or $1,000. **All subsequent years' savings are yours, with no fee to us.**

As my book was ready to go to press, we were notified by ZAPMYTAX that we had received another 10% reduction in our real estate taxes. What a great way to reduce expenses in our retirement years.

Veterans Exemptions

Veterans' exemptions from real estate taxes are not automatic; proper documents must be filed at the tax assessor's office for approval and hopefully acceptance by the taxing authority. In my case, I filed my applications as soon as I purchased my first house over 45 years ago and have had reductions in my real estate taxes that ranged from $1,000 to $2,500 a year. I figured that we saved in the neighborhood of about $80,000 over the period of time that we owned our two homes in New York. Not every municipality and state government is as generous to veterans as Suffolk County and the State of New York, so it's imperative to determine if your home qualifies for this generous exemption, which can save seniors a considerable amount of money over their homeownership years.

The website for the Department of Taxation and Finance in New York outlines some of the qualifications that are required and are probably common to other locations outside of New York, as follows:

> There are three different property tax exemptions available to veterans who have served honorably in the U.S Armed forces, which includes veterans of the U.S. Army, Navy, Air force, Marines, and Coast Guard.
>
> Whichever exemption a veteran chooses, it will apply only to county, city, town, and village taxes; it does not apply to school district and special district taxes.
>
> You can only receive one of the three exemptions listed below:

Alternative Veterans' Exemption

- Available only on residential property of a veteran who has served during a designated time of war, or who has received an expeditionary medal

- Currently is available in over 95% of the county, city, town, and village taxing jurisdictions across the state. The remainder may choose to offer this exemption in the future
- Veteran applicants should check with the assessor or clerk in the municipalities in which they reside to see whether the alternative veterans' exemption is offered

Cold War Veterans' Exemption

- Available only on residential property of a veteran who served during the Cold War period
- Counties, cities, towns, and villages have the option to offer this exemption to qualified veterans
- Check with your assessor or clerk to see whether the Cold War Veteran's Exemption is offered

Eligible Funds Exemption

- Provides a partial exemption
- Applies to property that a veteran or other designated person purchases. Such owners must purchase the property with military pensions, bonuses, or insurance monies.

As we can see from the above information, having a lifetime money-saving opportunity should not be taken lightly, and prospective and current veteran homeowners should be proactive in their search for saving money that could help them in having a more comfortable financial existence during their lifetime.

Reverse Mortgages

At last count, upward to a million senior citizens have taken advantage of reverse mortgages to help them enjoy, hopefully, a more secure financial journey during retirement. Up to 70% of the participants have opted, for better or worse, for "lump sum payments." We have not used this source of financing in our personal retirement plans, but many of our friends have, and I thought I would discuss exactly what some of the ramifications are of this type of financial planning that has become so popular with retirees. The following information explains briefly what these types of mortgages are about, and was taken in part from the Federal Trade Commission's (FTC) website where the full text can be seen and studied:

> If you're 62 or older and looking for money to finance a home improvement, pay off your current mortgage, supplement your retirement income, or pay for healthcare expenses, you may be considering a reverse mortgage. It's a product that allows you to convert part of the equity in your home into cash without having to sell your home or pay additional monthly mortgage bills. The FTC, the nation's consumer protection agency, wants you to understand how reverse mortgages work, the types that are available, and how to get the best deal.
>
> In a regular mortgage, you make monthly payments to a lender. In a reverse mortgage, you receive money from a lender, and generally don't have to pay it back for as long as you live in your home. The loan is repaid when you die, sell your home, or when your home is no longer your primary residence. The proceeds from these mortgages are generally tax-free, and many, but not all, have no income restrictions.
>
> There are three types of reverse mortgages:
>
> - **Single-purpose reverse mortgages** are offered by some state and local government agencies and nonprofit organizations.
> - **Proprietary reverse mortgages** are private loans that are backed by the companies that develop them.
> - **Federally-insured reverse mortgages,** which are known as Home Equity Conversion Mortgages (HECMs), are back by the U.S. Department of Housing and Urban Development (HUD)

and are the most popular mortgages that people over the age of 62 utilize.

Single-purpose reverse mortgages are the least expensive option. They are not available everywhere and can be used for only one purpose; for example, the lender might say the loan will be used for home repairs, improvements, or payment of property taxes. Most homeowners with low or moderate income can qualify for these loans.

HECMs and **proprietary reverse mortgages** may be more expensive than traditional home loans, and the upfront costs can be high. HECM loans are widely available, have no income or medical requirements, and can be used for any purpose. The amount you can borrow in either type of mortgage you select depends on several factors, including your age, the type of mortgage you select, the appraised value of your home, and current interest rates. In general, the older you are, and more equity you have in your home, and the less you owe on it, the more money you can get. **Proprietary loans** are useful if you own a higher-valued home; you may get a bigger loan advance from a commercial lender than from an HECM.

Reverse mortgage loan advances are not taxable, and generally don't affect your Social Security or Medicare benefits. You retain the title to your home, and you don't have to make monthly payments. The loan must be repaid when the last surviving borrower dies, sells the home, or no longer lives in the home as a principal residence. Because you retain title to your home, you are responsible for property taxes, insurance, utilities, fuel, maintenance and other expenses. If you don't pay these expense obligations,

your loan may become due and payable on demand by
the lender.

Beware of transactions that may be fraudulent or may be violating
the law. If you don't understand the cost or features of a reverse
mortgage or any other product offered to you, or if you are pressured
to close a deal right away, walk away from the deal or consider speaking
to a reverse mortgage consultant.

As previously mentioned, 70% of the borrowers of these mortgages
take lump-sum-payouts, and unfortunately deplete the funds sooner
than expected, leaving themselves short for the payment of real estate
taxes and the other home expenses that they are required to pay to
abide by the terms of their agreement with lenders. The latest statistics
indicate that 9.8% of reverse mortgages are currently delinquent in the
terms of their agreements and may be subject to foreclosures.

It is advisable that anyone contemplating using a reverse mortgage
in their retirement financial planning should contact a local HUD
office for a list of recommended counselors who are trained to help
prospective borrowers avoid some of the pitfalls that are prevalent in
the mortgage industry. They are also well versed in explaining how to
get the best deal from a lender; their telephone number is 1-800-569-
4297. Under current law, many of these loans require meeting with a
qualified consultant before an applicant will be considered.

Medical and Supplemental Insurance

The single most predominate concern of most senior citizens is the
cost of healthcare. Discussing the cost of **Medicare** and **Supplemental**
costs is like trying to maneuver through a **mine-field**, or in this case a
mind-field. Opinions are rampant, and trying to separate the politics
from the reality of health coverage is almost impossible. So when
the time came for me to decide what coverage I should have when I
became eligible for **Medicare** at age 65, I did some research and will
relate what my conclusions were that I hope will satisfy Barbara's and
my needs over the long run.

Medicare was established to help pay basic healthcare needs for people aged 65 and over, but was never intended to cover all medical expenses. In time, as life goes forward and our bodies require more and more attention, the cost of out-of-pockets dollars can become more than a person can afford. To help cover out-of-pocket medical costs, Medicare Supplemental Insurance can be purchased to help pay for items that are not covered by Medicare, such as:

- Medicare deductibles
- Hospital and medical care co-insurance
- Extended hospital care
- Physicians services, and hospital outpatients services and supplies
- Ambulance services

Additionally, with Medicare Supplemental insurance:

- **You can choose your own doctors—no need to select a primary care physician**
- No referrals are needed to see a specialist of your choice
- Virtually no claim forms to contend with, the insurance carrier takes care of all the paperwork
- Coverage is guaranteed renewable for the rest of your life

Of the above considerations, what was most important to us was being able to choose our own doctors, especially when we listed the doctors that we were already using for our various needs such as: cardiologists, oncologists, gynecologists, dermatologists, internists, neurologists, urologists, optometrists, and podiatrists. As we spend six months in New York and six months in Florida, the number of doctors that we required doubled. The thought of having a primary physician dictate to us what doctors we would have to use within their network when we needed a specialist's attention was totally unacceptable to our way of thinking, especially since we heard some of the horror stories from friends and relatives about the quality of service within their Home Maintenance Organization (HMO) networks, and in many instances, the unusually long waiting periods that they had before seeing specialists within their network. So after some in-depth research, we discounted contracting with any HMOs, although in many cases it was more cost effective than with a Medicare Supplemental Insurance company. As we had a good relationship with AARP as members, and used their services extensively for such things as travel information and vacation planning, drivers' education, getting retirement information on their website, movie discounts, hotel discounts, and any number of other services that we, as seniors and members, had easy access to on their website and by telephone, we narrowed our choices and decided to research using them as our Supplemental Insurance carrier.

It was a good choice, although it's more expensive than using HMOs. Over the last 15 years that I have been covered by AARP's Supplemental, and the 12 years that my wife has been in their plan, we have never been turned down for a choice of doctors that we needed for whatever ailed us, nor have we ever been dissatisfied with the quality of service that has been provided—and believe me, we have been seeing doctors regularly since our aging process seems to have accelerated with time.

With HMOs, a primary care physician is chosen and most of the services from the medical profession comes from their network and is dictated and supposedly monitored by a primary care physician. In our case, when we first went on Medicare, we contacted hospitals that we thought were the best in our neighborhood, called their doctors' advocacy service, and successfully chose a doctor that they recommended as our internist. As I'm a heart patient, having had bypass surgery in 1993, I also contacted St. Francis Hospital in Long Island, which is considered one of the best heart hospitals in the United States, and received a referral from them for a cardiologist. We still use the same physicians, and when we require a specialist, we ask our existing doctors who they think are the best in the field, and those are the doctors **we hire** to care for our problems. Mind you, doctors **we hire**: it's always our choice and not the choice of someone else with possibly different motives than ours. As an example, in 2001, I required carotid artery surgery. After speaking with my internist and cardiologist, they decided that the best hospital for the surgery was in New Hyde Park, Long Island. **I had a choice** of taking their advice or searching for another facility; **I took their advice**. Conversely, a neighbor of mine had the same problem around the same time; he had an HMO plan and was told by his primary care physician what hospital **he had to go to.** The hospital had one of the worst reputations on Long Island, but he decided to take the primary care physician's advice and had the procedure done there. There was a big difference: **my choice** was the best hospital for the procedure I needed, and **his doctor's choice** was based on a hospital within their network system, without any regard for their quality of service.

Our prescription drugs are also covered by our insurance plan with AARP, and if we stick to generics, where possible, medications usually cost from three to ten dollars per prescription. But if I choose not use generic drugs, then they can be purchased at a higher cost to me, but at a discounted rate.

A major problem that I've come across with our prescription drugs is where they are manufactured. It seems that CVS and Walgreens pharmacies have decided that the best medications for its customers are those made in India. They replaced some of our medications with those manufactured in that country without informing us, which put us into a frenzy as there have been recent newspaper articles stating that many drugs coming from India were not only tainted but in some cases possibly toxic. I had to call around to find a place that produced my high blood pressure medication from an acceptable country. Walmart Pharmacy had the medication and it was made in Israel, which to us is a better choice than India.

Of course, when we have prescriptions filed at CVS and Walgreens Pharmacies, we now ask what country they are manufactured in. If they can't provide us with the proper medication made in more acceptable countries, we will search for pharmacies that have a better source of drugs and transfer our prescriptions to them.

Annuities

Most of the following information was gleaned from Wikipedia websites and from my personal experience as a financial advisor.

Before purchasing an annuity, it's imperative that seniors consult with a competent financial advisor. An advisor will determine whether an annuity is a good overall choice in your retirement plans. One should think twice before using an insurance agent as an independent advisor that is promoting an annuity, as their interests may not always be entirely for the benefit of the retiree. There are many *Financial Advisor Guides* on the internet that can be helpful in choosing a qualified professional consultant.

Most people know what the basics of annuities are, but just to summarize:

> An annuity is a financial product that is commonly used in retirement planning. It's a contract with an insurance company where an investor agrees to pay a set amount of money, and in return the insurance company guarantees a certain number of payments, comprised of principal and interest, which will be received for a specific period of time or for the rest of an individual's life. The contract may or may not have life insurance provisions.
>
> Annuities are very popular among retirees as they can offer a steady stream of income with relatively little risk, if chosen wisely. It is important that retirees who choose annuities understand the complexities of investing in this kind of financial vehicle. Although it's often said that "Ignorance is Bliss," when it comes to annuities, ignorance can become a financial nightmare. According to annuity consultants *Annuity FY*:

> "There are over 2,000 insurance companies in the U.S. offering over 15,000 annuity products." To name just a few products that are available, I'll list just some of the more popular ones:
> - All Fixed
> - Immediate

- Deferred Income
- Fixed Indexed
- Fixed
- Secondary Market
- Equity Linked CDs

These are just the tip of the iceberg when it comes to the types of annuities that can be purchased, including a long list of Hybrids.

Sticking to the basics is what should concern retirees, and they are: **The Timing of Payments-Immediate or Deferred, Type of Investment, and Investment Liquidity:**

- **Timing of Payments-Immediate or Deferred**

  An **Immediate Annuity** is one in which payments begin immediately after a contract is signed and a lump sum is invested. This appeals to those who need immediate income from their annuities. There are a choice of payment methods, which could be from five to twenty years, which is typical, or for the rest of your life and your spouse's life, or any of the two. The investor can choose between fixed or variable payments. Interest earned is tax deferred until withdrawals begin.

  A **Deferred Annuity** allows for a lump-sum or installment payments to an insurance company. The payments from the insurance company are in the future at predetermined periods and usually starts at retirement. During the installment period, interest is accrued to the account tax free until withdrawals begin. These annuities are very popular and make up the majority of annuities in the United States.

- **Type of Investment-Fixed or Variable**

  A **Fixed Annuity** is considered a conservative investment as it provides the investor with a guaranteed rate of return derived primarily from government securities and high-grade corporate bonds. An example is, if a five percent interest rate is purchased, the investor will receive his investment back, plus five percent guaranteed interest. Insurance companies may sell additional and expensive coverage that will increase the percentage of return each year as a hedge against inflation on long-term contracts.

Variable Annuity

A variable annuity allows the investor to invest in various stock and bond portfolios and acts very much like a mutual fund. Due to the fact that investments are traded on the stock exchanges, their value can rise and fall based on their performance. As we can see, this means that there are no guaranteed fixed payments to the investor; as a matter of fact, there can be a reduction in the investor's account when the investments are doing poorly. The investor has a choice of funds ranging from conservative, such as money markets, fixed guaranteed accounts, and government bond funds, to more aggressive growth funds and even international funds. There are a myriad of choices for the investor which allows for diversification and in some cases, if wisely invested, a reduction in risk.

• **Investment Liquidity**

One of the primary concerns of people contemplating entering contracts for an annuity are the withdrawal options. There are two types: annuities with withdrawal penalties and without withdrawal penalties:

With Withdrawal Penalties

Most annuities have a surrender charge for amounts withdrawn above the agreed upon amounts in a contract. The question here is: Why would someone purchase a contract with a withdrawal penalty? Well, there are advantages and disadvantages; each involves how long contracts have been in force, when funds are withdrawn, and how much. Some insurance companies offer bonuses while others impose high penalties. It would be difficult to list the various choices, but what is important is to discuss with a financial advisor the advantages and pitfalls of contracts that have withdrawal penalties.

Without Withdrawal Penalties

Contracts without withdrawal penalties are allowed tax-fee exchanges with other annuities, regardless of the investor's age. No-surrender annuities do not have bonus features for early withdrawal, and some insurance companies even charge higher fees for their no-surrender charge products, so again, it's imperative that a financial advisor be involved with the purchase of any annuity contract.

There are two other areas of concern for retirees contemplating an annuity, they are **Death Benefits** and the prospective **Insurance Company's Financial Stability.**

Death Benefits

Everyone is concerned about what happens to their annuities when they die, and rightfully so. Does the value of annuities go to heirs? In most instances, the answer is yes, but there are exceptions. Fixed and Indexed Annuities paying lifetime income benefits generally do not have provisions for inheritance unless provided for in the contract. On the other hand, Variable Annuities usually always provide for inheritance unless there is no remaining value in the contract account.

So the question is, how much will your heirs inherit? With a Fixed Deferred Annuity, the value of the account will be distributed to heirs. But, the answer becomes complicated with Variable Annuities. Here are some of the death benefits with this type of annuity:

- **Standard Death Benefits,** which is defined as the current value of an annuity; this value may be fixed when the insurance company receives proof of the death of the insured, or the value may continue to change until the beneficiary makes a claim.
- **Return of Premium Death Benefits** are usually the greater of the premiums paid or the current value of the annuity, less any withdrawals and fees.
- **Stepped-up Death Benefits** are calculated the year after a contract is recorded and each year thereafter. The death benefit is then determined by the highest value on those anniversary dates, minus fees and withdrawals.

A beneficiary has different options for accepting death benefits. The options include payment of a lump sum, regular income payments, deferral of receiving death benefits, or taking over the ownership of the annuity contract.

As we can see, the insurance aspect of annuities can be beyond most people's comprehension, so again: **a financial advisor is a retiree's best friend when contemplating purchasing an annuity.**

Insurance Companies Financial Stability

Most people never consider the possibility of an insurance company going bankrupt and not having the ability to pay policyholders when the occasion arises. Fortunately, there are state guaranty associations and state-run funds that help pay claims if an insurance company is insolvent and can't meet its obligations. But, will the state agency make a policy holder or beneficiary whole? The answer is: in some cases yes and most cases no, as each state has a different reimbursement schedule for the insured.

Insurance companies are closely regulated and monitored, and in the event of a company getting into financial trouble, the State Guaranty Association will take over and probably try to find another insurance carrier to assume the responsibilities of the troubled company. If not successful, then they will reimburse the policy holders in accordance with the state's reimbursement schedule.

All the states, and the District of Columbia and Puerto Rico, have these associations and together they form the National Organizations of Life and Health Insurance Guaranty Associations (NOLHGA). The organization protects you in the event of an insurance company's insolvency as follows:

Most insurance companies, with few exceptions, that are licensed to write life and health insurance or annuities in a state are required to be members of the state's life and health insurance guaranty association. The provisions are:

- If a member company goes bankrupt, the state insurance associations will continue the coverage, pay the claims, and collect premiums due under the insurer's policies.
- Each State Insurance Association has a maximum amount that they will pay, which varies depending on the type of coverage and the states schedule of payments.
- A state guaranty associate will either pay claims directly or transfer policies to a financially stable insurance company.
- Guaranteed coverage amounts typically vary from $100,000–$500,000 in benefits, but it's wise to check your state to determine exactly what coverage it offers.

As we can see, it's important to investigate the financial condition of a prospective insurance company before deciding to purchase an annuity. This is one of the areas where a financial advisor can be useful when researching. It is comforting to know, when purchasing an annuity, that someone is acting on your behalf and his interest is for your benefit and not for the salesmen or insurance carriers.

Long-Term Care Insurance

People are duly concerned about the benefits and cost of long-term care for themselves and their families. When prolonged illness, disability, or injury befalls older individuals and they can no longer do ordinary tasks of everyday living or when their health requires constant day-to-day monitoring, they look to their family for support or to long-term insurance to provide them with comfort and security. According to the website, **CPA Site Solutions**, that caters to Certified Public Accounts, "About half of all nursing home expenses in the U.S. are paid for by patients and their families." Therefore, people should, sooner than later, consider the advantages of long-term care insurance while they are of sound mind and body, and when premiums are more affordable.

Although AARP does not provide for long-term care insurance, they have done a considerable amount of research on the topic to educate seniors. Their article *Understanding Long-Term Care Insurance*, by their Education & Outreach team, was published to educate the public, and will help clarify many confusing issues:

The basics of what you need to know
The phrase "long-term care" refers to the help that people with chronic illnesses, disabilities, or other debilitating conditions need on a daily basis over an extended period of time. The type of help needed can range from assistance with simple activities, such as, bathing, dressing and eating, to skilled care that's provided by nurses, therapists or other professionals.

Insurance policies offer many different coverage options. Since you can't predict what your future long-term care needs will be, you may want to buy a policy with flexible options. Depending on the policy options you select, long-term care insurance can help you pay for the care you need, whether you are at home, in an assisted living facility or nursing home. The insurance might also pay expenses for adult day care, care coordination and other services. Some policies will even help pay costs associated with modifying your **home so you can keep living in it safely.**

Factors to Consider

Your age and health: Policies cost less if purchased when you're younger and in good health. If you're older or have a serious health condition, you may not be able to get coverage—and if you do, you may have to pay considerably more.

The premiums: Will you be able to pay the policy's premiums—now and in the future—without breaking your budget? Premiums often increase over time, while your income may go down. If you find yourself unable to afford the premiums, you could lose all the money you've invested in the policy.

Your income: If you have difficulty paying your bills now or are concerned about paying them in the years ahead, when you may have fewer assets, spending thousands of dollars a year for a long-term care policy might not make sense. If your income is low and you have few assets when you need care, you might quickly qualify for Medicaid. (Medicaid pays for nursing home care; in most states it will also cover a limited amount of at-home care.) Unfortunately, in order to qualify for Medicaid, you must first exhaust almost all of your resources and meet their other eligibility requirements.

Your support system: Your may have family and friends who can provide some of your long-term care should you need it. Think about whether or not you would want their help and how much you can reasonably expect from them.

Your savings and investments: A financial advisor—or a lawyer who specializes in elder law or estate planning—can advise you about ways to save for future long-term care expenses and discuss the pros and cons of purchasing long-term-care insurance.

Your taxes: The benefits paid out through a long-term care policy are generally not taxed as income. Also, most policies sold today are "tax-qualified" by federal standards. This means if you itemize deductions and have medical costs in excess of 7.5 percent of your adjusted gross income, you can deduct the value of the premiums from your federal income taxes. The amount of the federal deductions depends on your age. Many states also offer limited tax deductions or credits. A fact to consider is that the federal government has recently raised the percentage for itemized deductions.

LONG-TERM POLICY SOURCES

Individual plans: Most people buy long-term care policies through an insurance agent or broker. If you go this route, make sure the person you're working with has had additional training in long-term care insurance (many states require it) and check with your state's insurance department to confirm that the person is licensed to sell insurance in your state.

Employer-sponsored plans: Some employers offer group long-term care policies or make individual policies available at discounted group rates. A number of group plans don't include underwriting, which means you may not have to meet medical requirements to qualify, at least initially. Benefits may also be available to family members, who must pay premiums and might need to pass medical screening. In most cases, if you leave the employer or the employer stops providing the benefit, you'll be able to retain the policy or receive a similar offering if you continue to pay the premiums.

Plans offered by organizations: A professional or service organization that you belong to might offer group-long-term care insurance policies. Just as with employer-sponsored coverage, study your options so you'll know what will happen if coverage is terminated or if you leave the organization.

State partnership programs: If you purchase a long-term care insurance policy that qualifies for the State Partnership Program, you can keep a specified amount of assets and still qualify for Medicaid. Most states have a State Partnership Program. Be sure to ask your insurance agent whether the policy you're considering qualifies under the program, and how it works with Medicaid, and when and how you would qualify for Medicaid. If you have more questions about Medicaid and the partnership program in your state, check with your State Health Insurance Assistance Program.

Joint policies: These plans let you buy a single policy that covers more than one person. The policy can be used by a husband and wife, two partners, or two related adults. However, there is usually a total or maximum benefit that applies to everyone insured under the policy. For instance, if a couple has a policy with a $100,000 maximum benefit and one person uses $40,000, the other person would have $60,000 left for his or her own services. With such a joint policy, you run the risk of one person depleting funds that the other partner might need in the future.

LONG-TERM POLICIES & PREEXISTING CONDITIONS

Insurers often turn down applicants due to preexisting conditions. If a company does sell a policy to someone with a preexisting condition, it often withholds payment for care related to that condition for a specified period of time after the policy is in force. Make sure that this period of withheld payments is reasonable for you if you are considering purchasing a policy with these conditions. **If you fail to notify a company of a previous condition, the company may not pay for any care related to that condition.**

Most companies will provide an informal review to determine whether you are eligible for a policy. This is helpful if you're likely to be denied coverage since another company may ask whether you've ever been turned down for coverage.

COVERED SERVICES

Some insurance companies require you to use services from a certified home care agency or a licensed professional, while others allow you to hire independent or non-licensed providers or family members. Companies may place certain qualifications—such as licensure, if available in your state—or restrictions on facilities or programs used. Make sure you buy a policy that covers the type of facilities, programs, and services you'll want and that are available where you live. (Moving to another area might make a difference in your coverage and the types of services available.)

Policies may cover the following care arrangements:

Nursing home: A facility that provides a full range of skilled health care, rehabilitation care, personal care, and daily activities in a 24/7 setting. Find out whether the policy covers more than room-and-board.

Assisted living: A residence with apartment-style units that makes personal care and other individualized services (such as meal delivery) available when needed.

Adult day care services: A program outside the home that provides health, social, and other support services in a supervised setting for adults who need some degree of help during the day.

Home care: An agency or individual who performs services, such as bathing, grooming, and help with chores and housework in your home.

Home modification: Adaptations, such as installing ramps or grab bars, to make your home safer and more accessible.

Care coordination: Services provided by a trained or licensed professional who assists with determining needs, locating services, and arranging for care. The policy may also cover the monitoring of care providers.

Full service options: If a new type of long-term care service is developed after you purchase insurance, some policies have the flexibility to cover the new services. The "future service" option may be available if the policy contains specific language about alternative options.

POLICY COVERAGE AMOUNTS AND LIMITS

Long-term care policies can pay different amounts for different services (such as $50 a day for homecare and $100 a day for nursing home care), or they pay one rate for any service. Most policies have some type of limit to the amount of benefits you can receive, such as a specific number of years or a total-dollar amount. When purchasing a policy, you select the benefit amount and duration to fit your budget and anticipated needs.

"Pooled benefits" allow you to use a total-dollar amount of benefits for different types of services. With this coverage option, you can combine services that meet your particular needs

To determine how useful a policy will be to you, compare the amount of your policy's daily benefits with the average cost of care in your area, and remember that you'll have to pay the difference. As the price of care increases over time, your benefit will start to erode unless you select inflation protection in your policy.

QUALIFYING FOR BENEFITS

"Benefit triggers" are the conditions that must occur before you start receiving your benefits. Most companies look to your inability to perform certain "activities of daily living" (ADLs) to figure out when you can start to receive benefits.

Generally, benefits begin when you need help with two or three ADLs. Requiring assistance with bathing, eating, dressing, using the toilet, walking, and remaining continent are the most common ADLs that trigger benefits. You should be sure your policy includes bathing in the list of benefit triggers because this is often the first task that becomes impossible to do alone.

Pay close attention to what the policy uses as a trigger for paying benefits if you develop a cognitive impairment, such as Alzheimer's disease. This is because a person with Alzheimer's may be physically able to perform activities but is no longer capable of doing them without help. Mental-function tests are commonly substituted as benefit triggers for cognitive impairments. Ask whether you must require someone to perform the activity for you, rather than just stand by and supervise you, in order to trigger benefits.

COVERAGE EXCLUSIONS

All policies have some conditions for which they exclude coverage. Ask your agent to review these exclusions with you. Most states have outlawed companies from requiring you to have been in a hospital or nursing facility for a specific number of days before qualifying for benefits. However, some states permit this exclusion, which could keep you from ever qualifying for a benefit.

Coverage exclusions for drug and alcohol abuse, mental disorders, and self-inflicted injuries are common. Be sure that Alzheimer's disease and other common illnesses, such as heart disease, diabetes, or certain forms of cancer aren't mentioned as reasons not to pay benefits.

WAITING AND ELIMINATION PERIODS

Most policies include a waiting or elimination period before the insurance company begins to pay. This period is expressed in the number of days after you are certified as "eligible for benefits," once you can no longer perform the required number of ADLs. You can typically choose from zero to up to 100 days. Carefully calculate how many days you can afford to pay on your own before coverage kicks in. (The shorter the period, the higher the price of the policy.)

Chose a policy that requires you to satisfy your elimination period only once during the life of the policy rather than a policy that makes you wait after each new illness or need for care.

Many policies allow you to stop paying your premium after you've starting receiving benefits. Some companies waive premiums immediately while others waive them after a certain number of days.

LONG-TERM CARE BENEFITS AND INFLATION

Since many people purchase long-term care insurance 10, 20, or 30 years before receiving benefits, inflation protection is an important option to consider. Indexing to inflation allows the daily benefit you choose to keep up with the rising cost of care.

You can increase your benefit by a given percent (5 percent is often recommended) with either compound or simple inflation protection. If you're under age 70 when you buy long-term care insurance, it's probably better to have automatic "compound" inflation protection. This means that the amount of your daily benefit increase will be based on the higher amount of coverage at each anniversary date of the policy. "Simple" inflation protection increases your daily benefit by a fix percentage of the original benefit amount. Typically, the simple option won't keep pace with the price of services.

In lieu of automatic increases, some policies offer "future-purchase options" or "guaranteed-purchase options." These policies often start out with more limited coverage and a corresponding lower premium. At a later, designated time, you have the option of increasing your coverage—albeit at a substantially increased premium.

If you turn down the option several times, you may lose the ability to increase the benefit in the future. Without increasing you coverage, this option may leave you with a policy that covers only a fraction of your cost of care. The younger you are when you buy long-term care insurance, the more important it is to buy a policy with inflation protection.

PREMIUM INCREASES AND POLICY CANCELLATIONS

Companies can't single you out for a rate increase. However, they can increase rates on a class of similar policies in your state. Most premiums do increase over the life of the policy. The National Association of State Insurance Commissioners has established rate-setting standards and about half of the states, along with several of the large insurance companies, have adopted these measures.

Long-term care policies are "guaranteed renewable," which means that they cannot be cancelled or terminated because of the policyholder's age, physical condition, or mental health. This guarantee ensures that your policy won't expire unless you've used up your benefits or haven't made your premiums payments.

PROBLEMS PAYING THE PREMIUMS

If you stop paying your premium or drop your benefit, a "nonforfeiture option" will allow you to receive a reduced amount of benefits based on the amount of money you've already paid. Some states require policies to offer nonforfeiture benefits, including benefit options with different premiums.

Since nonforfeiture provisions vary by location, check with your state's insurance department or your state's listing at the National State Health Insurance Assistance Program before dropping your policy. If your policy doesn't have a nonforfeiture option and you stop paying premiums, you'll lose all the benefits for which you have paid.

POLICY SHOPPING

If you've determined which long-term care insurance options best meet your needs and you're ready to buy a policy, do the following:

- Ask your state insurance department for a list of companies approved to sell long-term care insurance policies in your state. Find out whether there were complaints about any of the companies that sold them.
- Check the stability of the company and be sure it has a long history with this type of insurance. You can check this information at websites for companies including Moody's

Investors Service, Standard and Poor's, and A.M. Best.

- Compare information and costs from at least three major insurance companies. Find out how often and by how much the companies have increased their premiums.
- Get a written copy of any policy you're considering. Review it carefully, perhaps with the assistance of your attorney or financial advisor. Write out your questions and have a representative of the insurance company respond to your questions in writing.
- Never let anyone pressure or scare you into making a quick decision.
- Never pay any insurance premium in cash, and always make a check payable to the company and not an individual.
- Nearly all states require insurance companies to give you 30 days to review your signed policy. During this time, you can return a policy for a full refund if you change your mind.
- Still have questions or concerns? Contact the agency listed for your state at the State Health Insurance Assistance program.

Deciding whether long-term care insurance is right for you can take a significant amount of time and research, but making the effort will be time well spent.

AARP certainly did in-depth research to educate the public about the complications of choosing an acceptable and effective long-term care insurance policy. The only questions remaining are what are the pros and cons of purchasing a policy that can be very costly regardless of whether it's purchased early in a person's life or later on.

Fortunately, the CPA Site Solutions website also has an article *LONG-TERM CARE INSURANCE*, where they discuss the pros and cons of purchasing long-term care insurance. The full article can be seen on their web page www.cpasitesolutions.com. The following is a small part of their article on the subject:

THE PROS AND CONS

Long-term care insurance (LTCI) is both complex and controversial. Here is a summary of some of the main points **for** and **against** purchasing coverage.

Here are the reasons most often given by insured for purchasing LTCI

- To avoid being a burden to their families.
- To conserve assets for heirs.
- To be able to get into a nursing home of their choice.
- To be cared for at home as long as possible.
- To avoid Medicaid.
- To have peace of mind.

LTCI may not be the best way to achieve these goals as there are alternatives that may be more suitable for certain people.

Reasons for Buying LTCI

- Although expensive, it may provide protection against costly care. Thus, if other options are not viable, LTCI may be a way to meet your goal. Although LTCI policies remain a low-value product, they are better than nothing.
- If you have family caregivers, the extra home care coverage in LTCI might make it possible to remain at home longer.
- LTCI premium costs increase with age. Once you develop a serious medical condition, you probably will not qualify for coverage. Thus, it is better to buy LTCI early, if at all.

Reasons against Buying LTCI

- You cannot afford the premiums or don't have enough assets to protect.
- LTCI policies lack sufficient home care coverage to keep an individual out of a nursing home, unless family members or informal caregivers are available to help in providing care. Thus, if your goal is to avoid nursing homes at all costs, LTCI may not be the best way to go.
- LTCI policies return from 60% to 65% of total premiums paid in benefits. This return rate is much less than returns from other types of health insurance.

As we can determine from the above information of AARP's educational research and the CPA Site Solutions' pros and cons on the subject of LTCI, deciding whether or not to use insurance to provide for senior care is not an easy task. What we should keep in mind is that the average stay in a nursing home for seniors who are unable to care for themselves at the end of their life's journey, according to government information, is a little over two years. The average cost of a nursing home is between $4,000 and $5,000 a month, depending on the level of care and the location and quality of the facility of choice. So, let's multiply two-and-a-half years or 30 months by the upper average cost of a stay or $5,000 and we have a total of $150,000 cost when the average stay is reached. Keeping in mind that LTCI doesn't kick-in unless two or more daily functions can't be performed, the question to consider is how long one can expect to live if they can't perform, let's say, daily bathing, have trouble eating, are incontinent, or have trouble with memory issues?

The more we delve into LTCI, the more difficult it becomes to make a decision as to its usefulness. It seems to boil down to one's comfort level: if having LTCI gives you peace of mind and you can afford the premiums, than there is no doubt that it's the way to go.

CHAPTER SEVEN

Developing a Network of Doctors

To get the most out of retirement, and life in general, people should try to concentrate on their health issues as soon as possible. No one enjoys visiting a doctor's office, but a little bit of preventive maintenance can go a long way, especially during retirement. Having regular medical and dental checkups and following doctors' advice should become routine in our lives as we get older. Regular checkups and living a healthier life will go a long way to stretching Social Security benefits and annuity income that are based on longevity; the longer you live the more dough you get, which in turn will assure retirees more financial freedom and a better life. Of course, we can't predict what our health will be at any point in time, but taking precautionary steps certainly won't do anyone any harm, and in many cases may prevent serious illnesses from developing and changing the quality of our lives in our senior years. A simple annual flu shot and an extended pneumonia shot will go a long way in keeping those diseases from entering people's lives and possibly changing their futures into something they certainly didn't plan for when anticipating a good life during retirement. At the time of this writing, I'm a victim of shingles. It's been three months since I had the first signs of a rash and blistering, which disappeared in a couple of weeks. What I'm dealing with now is excruciating chest and back pain, for which I'm taking all kinds of pain killers to get by each day. Supposedly, if you have had chicken pox in your youth, chances are you will get shingles later on in life. I thought that I didn't have the pox, so never took a shingles shot, what a mistake. So, whether or not you have had chicken pox, it's wise to have the inoculation, as the older a person is when the virus rears its ugly head, the longer and more painful the ailment is likely to be. I'm hoping that before I finish this book, I'll be back to my normal easygoing person.

Paramount to maintaining good health is building a network of good doctors that have passed the test of time where our medical needs are concerned. We should develop relationships with doctors that are associated with the top hospitals in our area. **Never, never** choose a doctor or hospital based solely on the fact that they are conveniently located close to your home. I have known people who have done just that and didn't live to regret it (pun intended). In my experience, I've found that choosing a top hospital first and then getting recommendations from them usually resulted in our having doctors that have been with us for many years, who in turn have recommended other doctors associated with the top hospitals and who have cared for our medical needs far beyond our expectations. My wife and I, over the years, have accumulated a list of doctors that covers almost all the specialties: internists, cardiologists, dermatologists, oncologists, neurologists, urologists, optometrists, and gynecologists. What made our experience even more complicated was the fact that we are snowbirds and required doctors both in New York and in Florida. To round out our medical list, we had to locate dentists that were up-to-date with their treatments and the latest dental technology. It seems that Barbara and I spend an inordinate amount of time at the dentist trying to prolong the life or our rapidly decaying teeth with filings, root canals, bridges, caps, and implants. Having dentists with up-to-date equipment resulted in our spending less time in the dreaded treatment chairs, as X-rays and most other procedures were accomplished quickly. Unfortunately, most dentist visits aren't usually covered by Medicare or most Supplements, so getting your teeth shipshape if you have dental coverage prior to retirement is wise. If unable to acquire dental coverage during retirement, it is imperative to include the estimated cost of dental care when developing a budget, as it's one of the most expensive out of pocket costs that we have to deal with in our battle to retain the white pearls in our mouths during our senior years.

C H A P T E R E I G H T

Volunteering—"Paying it Forward"

I personally think that our "golden years" are the perfect time to share our good fortune with others. The fact that we reached retirement "without too many kinks in our armor" should give us an opportunity to "pay it forward." Paying back a little can be accomplished on a financial or a personal basis. I'm sure that during our lifetimes we in some way donated funds to religious and secular organizations, such as churches, synagogues, hospitals, and the many other worthy causes that are always in need of support. In retirement, when we have time available, many organizations that provide charitable and other essential services to the public could use our hands to help them in achieving their goals. What better way for senior citizens to contribute their time than to donate their precious talents for the betterment of the worthy goals of these useful organizations.

The essence of this book is to show by example, rather than by lecturing, how "old folks" can spend their time in a constructive and gratifying manner, and one of the ways is by volunteering time to worthwhile causes, preferably one that is dear to our hearts. In my case, the Salvation Army's Homeless Veterans Program caught my attention and eventually my time. I didn't seek out the program; as a matter of fact, I wasn't even aware that homeless veterans were an issue in the United States. My story starts with a visit to the Northport Veterans Medical Facility in Northport, Long Island for post-bypass surgery examinations and medication, which I was entitled to as a

Korean War veteran. I heard that the Salvation Army was considering setting up a homeless shelter and rehabilitation program and that our government was donating one of their vacant buildings at the huge complex to them for that purpose. I can't express how outraged I was in learning that we had veterans living on the streets of our neighborhood and that many were actually living in the woods on the facility's grounds in makeshift wooden shacks. I managed to get a meeting with the Salvation Army's leader of the program and asked what I could do to be of help. He explained that the program was to get vets off the streets for 90 days and provide them with food, shelter, and encouragement, and if possible, get them back into the workforce with meaningful jobs.

He gave me a tour of the huge vacant building, which was in dire need of repair. He explained his optimistic program in detail and his dream of having the government put the building in condition so he could begin hiring, furnishing, and, it was hoped, within a short period of time, getting veterans into the rest and rehabilitation program. He told me how important my volunteering would be to him as he was having a meeting with the neighborhood leaders to explain to them what the Salvation Army's plans were, and that my presence as a professional accountant and veteran would help him convince them that the homeless program would not be detrimental to them or their neighborhood.

One of the few experiences in my youth that I had had with the Salvation Army was during Christmas time when their soldiers, in full blue dress uniforms, invaded the streets of Manhattan and the entrances of major department stores with their donation kettles and bell ringing. A very vivid encounter with their soldiers was when I was in the United States Air Force. At each embarkation point that I shipped out of, they were there serving coffee, cake, and good cheer to the airmen going overseas. Other than during the holidays and my military experience, the only other experience I had with them was when the musical film *Guys and Dolls* came out in 1959, which I saw several times. It starred Marlon Brando as Sky Masterson, a high-ranking gambler, and Frank Sinatra as Nathan Detroit, a low-ranking gambler. What they both had in common was making a fast buck, and their way of getting some quick and safe dough was by conning the Salvation Army's Sergeant Sarah Brown, played by the beautiful actress Jean Simmons, into allowing them to use her facility as a cover for their gambling operations. Up until my agreeing to join the Army's homeless shelter program, all of my memories of the organization were pleasant ones, so I went head over heels into the project of assisting in getting the homeless shelter up and running.

I think a little history from their archives about the organization is in order for those who might be interested in volunteering in their outreach programs:

> The Salvation Army began in 1865, when William Booth, a London minister, gave up the comfort of his pulpit and decided to take his message into the street where it would reach the poor and homeless, the hungry and the destitute. His original plan was to send the street converts to established churches, but he soon realized that the poor did not feel comfortable or welcome in the pews of most of the churches and chapels of Victorian England. Regular churchgoers were appalled when these shabbily dressed, unwashed people came to join them in worship. So he decided to found a church especially for them—the East London Christian Mission. Although the mission grew slowly, his faith in God remained undiminished.
>
> By the early 1900s, the Army spread around the world. It soon had officers and soldiers in 36 countries, including the United States. This well-organized, flexibly structured organization inspired a great many much-needed services such as: women's social work, the first food depot for the poor, the first day nursery, and the first Salvation Army hospital. During World War II, they operated over 3,000 service units for the armed forces, which led to the formation of the USO. Today, the organization is stronger and more powerful than ever. Now, in over 106 nations around

the world, they continue to work where the need is greatest, guided by faith in God and love for all people. In 2010, over 3 million volunteers gave of their time, talents, and resources to assist the organization's goal of "Doing the most good for everyone in need."

So I became one of the many volunteers of the astonishing Army as a civilian representative on the Neighborhood Committee, which had periodic meetings to keep the people in the surrounding area abreast of what the Army was accomplishing and to act as a sounding board for any complaints from either side. I was also a representative of the Suffolk County Veteran's Committee, whose main purpose was overseeing the welfare and care of the homeless veterans. We met once a month to discuss the progress of the Army's programs and contributed our advice to them based on our experiences in the military. We helped resolve many of the issues that they were having with the unfortunate veterans, especially the Viet Nam Vets, who seemed to think that the world was against them, and that they were the bad guys. Two of our primary goals were to raise funds to build a kitchen and laundry room that would make the shelter self-sufficient and would introduce the patients to working in those environments as cooks, waiters, machine maintenance men, etc. By accomplishing our objectives, the patients would again join others in productive endeavors and hopefully be helped to regain their self-confidence and composure as civilized human beings. Our group of volunteers accomplished our goals and much more. We not only raised enough funds for the kitchen and laundry room, but we also supplied the furniture for their small dining area, TV lounge, exercise room, and library.

The satisfaction that I received while working with fellow veterans, and in some small way contributing to their reentry into useful lives, remains one of the highlights of my life.

While I was busy with my various charitable endeavors, my wife Barbara donated her time and knowledge as a Council Member Overseer at the Tilles Center for the Performing Arts, which is located on the C.W. Post Campus of Long Island University in Brookville, Long

Island, NY. The Center's Concert Hall seats over 2,500 theatergoers and features orchestral performances, fully staged operas, ballets, and modern dance, along with Broadway shows, and all forms of music, dance, and theater from around the world. Chamber music, cabaret, solo recitals, and theater productions for children and adults are presented in their more intimate 500-seat Hillwood Recital Hall. They host more than 100 performances a year by world-renowned artists in music, theater, and dance. Among the artists and ensembles that have been presented by the Center are the Boston Symphony Orchestra conducted by Seiji Ozawa, cellist Yo-Yo-Ma, violinist Itzhak Perlman, the Big Apple Circus, Bill Cosby, James Taylor, Liza Minnelli, and the Met Orchestra with James Levine. In addition, Tilles Center is home to important regional arts organizations including the Long Island Philharmonic and Eglevsky Ballet.

What got Barbara interested in the Council was her love of music, especially classical. In her formative years, she studied piano and classical guitar for ten years, and continued with her passion well into retirement. As a Council Overseer, she attends meetings that review the programs and progress of Tilles Center. The President of Long Island University, David Steinberg, heads the early morning meetings and lends his energy and talent to all the discussions. Fund raising for the Center is usually one of the main topics. It seems that performing arts can only exist today by the donations of generous sponsors and the many volunteers who donate their time as ushers, guides, or whatever jobs are necessary to keep the venue performing at its peak.

A major endeavor of the Council is to introduce classical music to children with the hope that they will become the music lovers of the future. Its popular "Swing for Kids" program is funded by an annual golf and tennis tournament that takes place at "Meadow Brook Club" in Jericho, and the "Creek Golf Course" in Locust Valley, Long Island. The annual tournament benefits Arts Education, which includes the "Swing for Kids" program. The effort is primarily run by senior volunteers who are devoted music lovers and enjoy being a part of programs that they are passionate about.

Peter Tilles, one of the leaders of the program, made the following statement at a meeting we attended:

With funds provided by "Swing for Kids" over the years, Tilles Center for the Performing Arts has been able to strengthen its commitment to the artists and audiences of tomorrow. As part of the arts education program, thousands of school children participate in master classes, in-school workshops, and performances at Tilles Center by world-class artists renowned for their multicultural work in classical music, jazz, dance, theater, and opera. Additionally, through Tilles Center's residency program with the New York Philharmonic, young musicians have an opportunity to work with Philharmonic soloists in rehearsals, master classes, and panel discussions. The Center's "Arts Start Here" program introduces youngsters to live performances by highly acclaimed artists from the world of dance, music, and theater. The ambitious Arts Education Program, modeled on the prestigious Lincoln Center Institute for Arts in Education Program, provides Long Island school districts with high-caliber weekday performances which support and expands schools' curricula through the use of study guides, in-school workshops, and extensive teacher training. Tilles Center strives to nurture the audiences and the visual and performing artists of tomorrow through such outreach activities as "Performances for Schools," "Tilles Scholars," an annual residence program with the New York Philharmonic and regular student art exhibitions.

These programs are successful thanks to the many **volunteers** who devote their time and energy to enhancing and sustaining the Performing Arts.

Two popular volunteer organizations that many retirees are active in are the **Smithsonian Institute** and its extensive museum network and the **Memorial Sloan-Kettering Hospital** organization. A little information about them may interest readers as they are representative of other associations that have volunteer opportunities available on a local and national level.

Volunteers have provided a primary means of support for the Smithsonian since its establishment in the mid-19th century. Strong volunteer partnerships are essential for the Institution to successfully carry out its work. Some of the opportunities are:

- **Docent Programs** – Docents are volunteer guides who provide group learning experiences in the form of museum tours, demonstrations, or instructions in special activity areas.
- **Museum Information Desk Program** – Volunteers in this program work at a museum information desk where they are on the front lines interacting with visitors of all ages on a daily basis.
- **Telephone Information Program** – These volunteers handle public inquiries from around the world on all aspects of the Smithsonian's activities, administrative functions, and services.
- **Special Support Programs** – Offers volunteers an opportunity to enhance the museum experience for visitors in various ways, from assisting with hands-on activities to providing the staff with administrative support.
- **Citizen Science** – Offers special opportunities to assist in the various research programs.
- **Behind-the-Scenes Volunteer Program** – Offers challenging alternatives to public-oriented volunteer activities. Opportunities are generally available in: archives; libraries; administrative offices; conservation laboratories; and curatorial divisions related to art, history, and science collections.
- **Seasonal Programs** – Includes summer opportunities including the Smithsonian Folklife Festival, which is presented for a two-week period during the summer. This endeavor relies upon the services of hundreds of volunteers who assist with every aspect of the annual celebration including folk crafts, music, food, and culture. For more information email info@

si.edu. The opportunities at the Smithsonian are endless for volunteers. The same email address will get information on volunteer activities at the Smithsonian Zoo and the Institute's locations around the country.

I was introduced to the Memorial Sloan-Kettering organization under very unhappy circumstances. In my younger days, when my hair was noticeably red, I was guilty of spending too much time at Coney Island Beach lying in the sun with no hat and only the hair on my head, arms, and legs protecting my very light skin. The expression "Play today, pay tomorrow" is certainly the case with skin cancer. My many visits to their Hauppauge, Long Island, facility to get rid of the unwelcomed visitors on my body made me realize their importance in body cancer preventive maintenance, and the organization's "cutting edge" research and technology. The institute has a unique volunteer program, which is outlined on their website www.mskcc.org as follows:

> Since its establishment more than 60 years ago, Memorial Sloan-Kettering's Department of Volunteer Resources has grown to include many participants who donate a combined 75,000 hours of service per year.
>
> The volunteer department is an integral part of the culture of the organization. Our volunteers provide services that enhance the quality of life in the hospital through activities ranging from transporting patients to staffing the Thrift Shop.
>
> We also offer several specialized volunteer opportunities. Cancer survivors treated at Memorial Sloan-Kettering and their caregivers may participate in the "Patient-to-Patient Support Program." Volunteers with writing backgrounds can share their expertise with patients through the "Visible Ink Program." In addition, those who have certified therapy dogs can interact with patients through the "Caring Canine Program."

Alongside outstanding medical care, volunteers' humanity and spirit are at the core of the organization. Our volunteers vary in age and background, from high school students fulfilling service requirement to employed and retired adults wishing to give back to the community. Each member of our dynamic group is committed to providing a welcoming and compassionate environment for patients, families, and visitors.

Volunteers serve at least three hours per week and must maintain a good attendance record. Though we accept volunteers for all shifts, our greatest need is for those who can work Monday through Friday between the hours of 9:00 AM to 5:00 PM. Our adult volunteers generally commit to at least one year of service, while the average tenure of a volunteer is more than two years; some continue to serve for decades.

Throughout the United States, it's estimated that over 63 million Americans will donate their time to various organizations this year for an average of 34.2 hours a year, providing $163 billion worth of services, free of charge. So if any readers are feeling bashful or uneasy about volunteering, they shouldn't. Just ask your neighbors—I'm sure you'll find many of them are already donating their time at churches, hospitals, museums, and art centers. Two good websites to explore for volunteer opportunities are: www.mygooddeed.org and www.serve.gov.

C H A P T E R   N I N E

Should Seniors Join AARP?

I would imagine that many of my readers are members of AARP and don't need coaching from me about the organization. But for those who are not members, or those who are not aware of the many benefits that being a member provides, I think that my experience with AARP might be helpful, and will possibly encourage nonmembers to join the 50+ organization.

I remember so clearly the bombardment of mail I received from AARP as I approached my 50th birthday. The fact that I refused to admit to myself, and to others, that I was approaching that milestone age, caused me to discard many of the invitations without opening the envelopes. But as time passed, and my hair grayed and slowly disappeared, I started reading the information that was presented and figured that for a small membership fee of $16 a year, which when the time came would include my wife Barbara, how could I possibly go wrong by joining? So I filled out the application and became a bona fide member of the 30+ million senior citizens' organization. Today, filling in membership information can be done online on their website and gives prospective members immediate membership for a very small fee.

The benefits of being a member are quite numerous, so I will only list a small portion of them and then go on to discuss how some of the benefits were advantageous to me and my darling wife, Barbara. I would also like to emphasis that their political views were never a

— 206 —

consideration in my joining the organization, as many of them are controversial and have nothing to do with the benefits that I thought would be useful to me in my retirement.

From their enormous website, I gathered some information I thought might be useful:

> AARP is a nonprofit, nonpartisan membership organization for people age 50 and over. It's dedicated to enhancing the quality of life for all as they age. We lead positive social changes and deliver value to members through information, advocacy, and service.
>
> AARP also provides a wide range of unique benefits, special products, and services for our members. Some are:
>
> - **Benefits, Discounts**—includes access to health, automobile, and homeowners insurance, in addition to other services. We offer great discounts on travel, online services, including dating, telephone support, and much more. Some widely used discounts are: 15% discounts at Outback Steakhouse and Bonefish restaurants, 30% off one-year membership at Ancestry.com, 10% off entire purchases at Anna's Linens, and 45% off of the first year's membership at AngiestList.com.
> - **Advocacy Information**—provides a voice in Washington and in your state, representing you on issues like Medicare, Social Security, and consumer safety.
> - **Valuable information on Living Well**—helps you learn more about healthy living, financial planning, consumer protection, and caring for parents.
> - **Award-winning Publications**—AARP *The Magazine* is packed with exciting features,

and the *AARP Bulletin,* which is also available online, brings you the latest pertinent news and information every month.

- **Community Services**—includes access to local chapters, driver safety courses, and a nationwide volunteer network.

More information on AARP Benefits—members receive a bimonthly magazine that addresses the needs and concerns of the 50+ population, including the 76 million strong baby boomer generation. The magazine covers a broad range of topics, including health, finance, and leisure. Members can also receive the *AARP Bulletin,* which is published 11 times a year and is packed with news and practical information, an online version of this newsletter in available and covers such topics as health issues, online dating, national and state legislation effecting seniors, just to name a few of its useful topics.

An AARP program that we have been taking advantage of for over 15 years is their **Driver Safety Course.** What attracted us to the course was the 10% savings on automobile insurance that is available to residents of New York who complete the course and receive a Certificate of Completion, which is submitted to a member's insurance company and is good for three years, resulting in a savings for us of $1,800. Doing the arithmetic, we can see that we have saved over $9,000 since we took advantage of the driving courses. Members that take the course should check with their insurance carriers to see what discounts are available in their home states. We have also received an insurance discount from our Florida insurance company since we became snowbirds, which has added another $2,000 to $9,000 savings.

After gloating over the savings, we realized that the course also offered very important safety instructions, especially for seniors that are getting on in years or have physical limitations, as they have courses that are geared to older citizens that have restricted movements or other more serious disabilities. AARP provides a website **Why Take a**

Driver Safety Course? Some of the beneficial information to seniors that can be found there follows:

> By taking a driver's safety course, you'll learn the current rules of the road, which may be somewhat different than when you took your driver's test. You'll also learn defensive driving techniques, and how to operate your vehicle more safely in today's increasingly challenging driving environment. You'll learn how you can manage and accommodate age-related changes in vision, hearing, and reaction time. In addition, you'll learn:

- How to minimize the effect of dangerous blind spots
- How to maintain the proper following distance behind another car
- The safest ways to change lanes and make turns at busy intersections
- Proper use of safety belts, air bags, anti-lock brakes, and new technologies used in cars
- Ways to monitor your own and others' driving skills and capabilities
- The effects of medications on driving
- The importance of eliminating distractions, such as eating, smoking, and cell-phone use

> After completing the course, you will have a greater appreciation of the driving challenges and how you can avoid potential collisions and injuries to yourself and others.

> The course is available in classroom and online settings and will probably qualify you for insurance discounts, so consult your agent for details. You might also be eligible to receive a discount on roadside assistance plans.

The classroom course costs only $12 for members and $14 for non-members. The cost for the online course is $15.95 for members and $19.95 for non-members.

Some of the courses also qualify drivers that receive a Certificate of Completion and the opportunity to have points removed from their drivers' licenses. All and all, it's not a bad way to spend, or should I say **invest,** $16 to become a member of an organization that is geared to enhancing senior citizens well-being.

Life Reimagined

This is a unique program that AARP offers to members who would like to explore possible life changing goals. The program is best explained by their press release of May 28, 2013:

> **AARP Launches Life Reimagined to Offer Ways from Discovering New Possibilities and Navigating "What's Next?"**
>
> *Single source of online/offline tools and experiences offer a unique step-by-step approach to achieving goals and dreams at any age.*
>
> **Press release - Washington** - Life Reimagined, launched today by AARP, is the first-of-its-kind series of online and offline experiences that guide people through life's transition by helping them discover new possibilities and connect with a community of people pursuing similar passions and goals.
>
> With people living longer and redefining traditional notions of aging and retirement, a new life stage has emerged. Today, many people in their 50s, 60s, and beyond are choosing to add these years in the middle versus tacking them on later in the "winding down stage."
>
> "AARP understands how important it is for people to set and achieve goals at any age," said Emilio Pardo,

AARP executive vice president and chief brand officer. "They are looking for tools, guidance, and connections to help them regain choice and control in their lives and discover a path to personal fulfillment. We built Life Reimagined to open doors and fill the gap to available resources, to ultimately help people live their best lives."

Life Reimagined online centers on an exclusive, customizable roadmap, available at www. lifereimagined.org, that helps people understand where they are in their journey to achieve their goals and dreams, reflect, and make decisions in planning their next steps. It also includes a Sounding Board—a new kind of private social network for people to surround themselves with trusted friends and allies. Through the Sounding Board and other connection tools, members of the Life Reimagined community help each other by offering advice and support to help reach their goals, both big and small.

Life Reimagined is powered by the Life Reimagined Institute for Innovation, a world-class group of thought leaders in the areas of life and career coaching, psychology, personal development, health and entrepreneurship.

As part of Life Reimagined, AARP announced its newest ambassador–nineteen-time Grammy Award-winning musician, producer, and entrepreneur, Emilio Estefan. Estefan will share his personal experience and expertise on a variety of subjects, including his passion for living, mentoring, entrepreneurship, philanthropy, and much more. "I feel a very personal connection to Life Reimagined," said Emilio, AARP's Life Reimagined Ambassador. "It's been nearly 40 years since I started my first band, so reimagining life is in my soul, and I want to remind people that there are no age limits on setting and achieving goals. For me, being the Life

Reimagined Ambassador is about helping people to see that their dreams really can come true, regardless of who they are, where they were born or what they're doing today."

AARP is also pleased to announce that Nancy Perry Graham has been appointed Executive Producer, Digital Media for Life Reimagined. For the past five years, Nancy has been the Editor-in-Chief of *AARP The Magazine* and for the prior five years served as the magazine's Deputy Editor.

So, here we have a program that can help people become *rewired*, regardless of their ages. It gives them a chance to experiment with life changing dreams that could very well become opportunities to begin life anew, not out of necessity, but out of choice.

AARP has come up with a novel approach to exploring opportunities for seniors before they retire. They use a deck of playing cards with corresponding pictures that gives the player insight into some of the choices that are available to retired folks who desire to find their new calling in life. Some of the cards that I investigated were:

- Building Relationships
- Resolving Disputes
- Adding Humor to One's Life
- Growing Things
- Selling Intangibles
- Awakening Spirit
- Organizing Things
- Translating Things
- Straightening Things Up

I counted 44 cards in their library. They suggest that starting with five cards should get a person going. Their promotion states:

It's easy—just look through the deck of cards and select what you like doing most. Are you more creative or analytical? Do you like building things or building relationships? This activity will help you focus in on what you love to do and provide insights into your personality type.

When you combine what you enjoy with what you're good at, you can move your life forward with more purpose and satisfaction. Life Reimagined helps you take the first step with **Find Your Calling**, one of the many activities designed to guide you towards what's next.

I had lots of fun exploring and imagining how I would conduct myself in many of the suggested opportunities that the cards outlined. It certainly would have been exciting for me if the program had been available prior to my retiring over 15 years ago. It would have been enjoyable to explore the many possibilities offered through the playing-card game that is now available through AARP's Life Reimagined.

Playing the card game will certainly assist people contemplating retirement in determining how they plan to rewire themselves for possibly the best remaining part of their lives.

C H A P T E R   T E N

Preparing a Will and Other Important Documents

Those of us who had the courage when we were young to deal with documents that concerned death, probably already have a will. But there are many who wait until they are sick or are threatened with the possibility of death before they put pen to paper and outline what they want to happen to their assets after their demise. There are no laws that state that you have to make a will or estate plans, but there are laws that dictate what will happen to your assets if you do not take advantage of your right to determine the distribution of your wealth in the form of a will.

If you do not have a will, your state of residence will determine who will get your assets. Many states have different formulas, but generally, your wealth will be split between close relatives, including the cousin that you hate. If you have no close relatives, then your estate may go to a relative that you didn't know existed. If you have no living relatives, then the state becomes your "long-lost uncle" and the recipient of your hard-earned assets. It is a mistake to think that you will save money by not having a will or trust set up to protect your wealth after your demise. It is always costly to rely on the good intentions of a state since it may not be able to easily determine who all your heirs are and will have to spend an inordinate amount of your money to find heirs and satisfy the intentions of the state laws.

While the search for relatives goes on, money that is usually needed by the immediate family is tied up until the legalities of the state laws are satisfied. Through the state-made will process, everything may be held in abeyance while attempts are made to find heirs, post bonds, marshal assets, and prepare the necessary accounting documents that are required by the state to move forward with the lawful accumulation and distribution of an estate's assets. Let's not forget federal and state estate taxes that might have to be paid at the top tax brackets if there is no will.

In addition to the distribution of assets, there are many other problems of not having a will. One example is, a widowed grandmother dies in a car crash with her only living adult relative, her daughter, and has no will. Her daughter has two minor children whose futures, according to law, will be dictated by the state until they reach maturity. The state will appoint a person or institution to care for the children and to manage the grandparent's wealth. When the grandchildren reach legal age, usually 18, any assets that remain will be distributed to them. I'm sure that no one wants a state to determine how their wealth is disbursed or how minor children are cared for until their maturity. Fortunately, there is an alternative to the state-made will, which simply requires preparing a will of your own—hopefully, while you are still young and healthy. With a valid will, trust, and other documents, such as electing beneficiaries in life insurance policies and retirement plans, you decide who receives the fruits of your labor and not the state.

Keep in mind that preparing a will is not only an emotional event, but one that requires the assistance of qualified professional accountants and lawyers. An example of an **emotional will** can be found in the recent newspaper headlines **"Gandolfini's $70 million estate owes the government approximately 70% in estate taxes."** The famous actor who played the New Jersey mafia boss, Tony Soprano, in the popular television series *The Sopranos* was wise enough to prepare a will while he was young, at age 51, and in complete control of his faculties. **But**, there was certainly something lacking in his choice of the professionals that he used to prepare his will in a manner that should have satisfied his emotional concerns and protected his estate from paying unnecessary federal and state estate taxes. The highlight of his problem was that he wanted to provide for his family in a fair manner, evidently without any consideration for estate taxes.

His will had somewhat simple provisions. After giving $1.6 million to friends and relatives and making provisions for his personal property and his house and land in Italy, he split the remainder of his estate among four people: 30% to each of his two sisters, 20% to his present wife, and 20% to his daughter. His son received the proceeds of a life insurance policy that wasn't subject to estate taxes. As simple and ordinary as these provisions might seem, he missed an opportunity in estate planning terms by leaving only 20% of his estate to his wife as there is an unlimited deduction for estate tax purposes for gifts made to a surviving spouse. The use of a marital and other trusts can usually take advantage of the marital deduction while still ensuring that children will eventually receive the bulk of the estate. Although trusts can be tricky, with the assistance of **qualified professionals**, the proper trusts would have cut tens of millions of dollars from his estate tax bill.

It seems that what the IRS couldn't get from the mafia boss Tony Soprano, it made up for, due to the poor tax planning on the actor's and his financial professionals' part. No one likes to contemplate death, but the expensive lesson that the IRS is about to teach the Gandolfini family is one that can be avoided by most seniors with a little common sense planning and the aid of qualified professionals.

He is not the only rich or famous person that was snagged by the taxing authorities or left money to people that they didn't even know because of poor estate planning. According to the Premier Financial Services at www.sklenar.com, the following are some of the others who didn't tax advantage of estate tax strategies:

> **Marilyn Monroe** sadly took her life in 1962 and left the rights to her licensing and royalty deals to her acting coach, Lee Strasberg. Today, those royalties generate millions of dollars a year. The odd thing is that they're enriching a woman that Monroe never

met, as Strasberg left them to his third wife, in 1982. She subsequently sold the rights for an estimated 20 to 30 million dollars. Marilyn also left in her will $100,000 in a trust to support her mother. With no other estate plans or trusts in place, royalties and licenses that she wanted to be given to charitable causes never materialized. Debts and Federal Estate Taxes caused a 55% shrinkage in her net estate.

Elvis Presley, the king of rock "n" roll, didn't have good tax saving advice so his ten million dollar estate had a shrinkage of 73%, resulting in a net estate of 2.7 million dollars.

Some other famous or rich people that didn't have adequate estate tax planning and paid exorbitant taxes are:

Howard Hughes—Famous aviator/industrialist/film producer/ eccentric.

Warren E. Burger—Former Chief Justice of the United States Supreme Court.

John Denver—Singer/Songwriter.

Walter Cronkite—Beloved broadcaster.

John D Rockefeller, Sr.—Founder of Standard Oil Co., Industrialist and Philanthropist.

Clark Gable—Screen Star.

You can visit Premier Financial Services' website at www.sklenar. com, for a listing of other famous dignitaries and more information on the ones that are listed above.

With the help of a competent attorney specializing in estate planning, a will can be prepared to satisfy a person's after-death wishes. A major consideration to discuss with your lawyer is the amount of taxes that must be paid upon your death and how to provide for the cash to meet those obligations. Gift and estate taxes are not usually a primary concern at the beginning of the preparation of a will, but after all the bequests are made, the subject becomes the second most important one, as no one wants to pay more than their fair share of taxes. Remember there are no laws against legal tax avoidance, especially if directed by competent and honest advisors.

Dealing with the emotional side of preparing a will can be eased and can satisfy tax considerations if parents communicate to their heirs what is expected of them and what they can expect when the final event occurs. Keep in mind that estate planning is not a democratic process; it's the parents' wishes. But it's wise to let the kids know approximately what they can expect after the reading of a will. One of the most perplexing questions is: should all the children be treated equally? Experts say that it certainly helps, but as we saw in the Gandolfini will, being fair will probably cost his heirs tens of millions of dollars in unnecessary taxes that should have been kept by them.

Of course, to minimize squabbling, leaving inheritances to kids as equally as possible would be ideal, but that is rarely the case, so make sure that the uneven distribution of your assets go with an explanation such as, "Sister Jane is getting the house because she was our caregiver when we needed assistance, or brother John is getting most of our investments because he is in need of financial support while the rest of our children are financially self-sufficient." This philosophy also applies to assigning responsibilities of settling your affairs. Keep in mind that when you appoint responsibility you're making a statement as to who is worthy, capable and who you trust. It's important to be concerned about people's feelings, so lay out your plans in advance and explain to the kids why you made your choices, which in many cases may not include assigning any financial responsibilities to them.

Many people feel uncomfortable about speaking to their children about their wills and why they made unequal distribution choices financially and for their reasons of choosing those who will oversee their estate. So, at the very least, notes should be written to go along with the wills that might say something like, "We love you all equally. Here are the reasons we made our choices and hope no one is offended. . . ."

In my experience as a Certified Public Accountant and financial advisor, I found that wills with incentive clauses usually create more problems than they solve. The popular phrase is "Don't try to control someone from the grave." These documents stipulate that heirs inherit only if they perform certain acts, such as, "Johnny must graduate college before . . . or Shelia must complete a drug rehabilitation program and be drug free for. . ." These types of provisions can create hard feelings and can lead to the beneficiaries suing the trustee and depleting the estate's assets in needless lawsuits.

Finally, if you want siblings to inherit equally when it comes to life insurance, never put down one child with instructions that the proceeds should be shared equally. It's wise to make all the siblings beneficiaries so that they will receive their respective shares upon settling with insurance companies. Moreover, when it comes to jewelry, art, or other items to bequeath, always leave a list of who gets what, along with the method of dividing up whatever is left. It's wise that beneficiaries know in advance what is being left to them to avoid conflicts when it's time to distribute personal effects. It's also wise to attach a list to your will detailing exactly who gets personal property and giving a copy of the list to your beneficiaries.

After the details of a will have been ironed out, then the last decisions that must be made are choosing an executor (male) or executrix (female), and a trustee to handle any tax saving trusts that might be beneficial to the beneficiaries and satisfy tax saving opportunities. The duties of each person can be summarized as follows:

> **An executor or executrix's** duties are to oversee and execute the wishes of the deceased that are expressed in a will. Typically, he or she is the person responsible for making sure the will is offered to probate. Their duties also include disbursing property to beneficiaries as designated in a will, obtaining information of

potential heirs, collecting and arranging for payments of debts of the estate, and approving or disapproving creditor's claims. An executor will make sure estate taxes are calculated, that necessary tax forms are filed in a timely manner, and that appropriate payments are made to the taxing authorities. In most cases, they are the representatives of the estate for all purposes, and have the ability to sue and be sued on behalf of the estate. They hold legal title to estate property, but may not use the title or property for their own benefit, unless permitted by the terms of a will. In large estates, this person or persons are paid fees. It's wise to state in the will what those fees are, as this will avoid disagreements between the executors and the beneficiaries.

A trustee is the person that oversees tax saving trusts that are properly set up, such as:

Irrevocable trusts—the assets in it are no longer yours once the trusts are set up, and typically you can't make changes without the beneficiary's consent. The appreciated assets in the trusts aren't subject to estate taxes.

Credit shelter trusts—with this type of trust (also called a bypass or family trust), you write a will bequeathing an amount to the trust up to but not exceeding the estate tax exemption. Then you pass the rest of your estate to your spouse tax-free. And there's an added bonus: once money is placed in the bypass trust, it is forever free of estate tax, even as it grows. **Generation-skipping trusts**—also called a dynasty trust, allows you to transfer a substantial amount of money tax-free to beneficiaries who are at least two generations your junior—typically your grandchildren.

Again, I must emphasize that it's imperative that professionals handle the preparation of wills and the other important documents that are necessary to satisfy your wishes and to minimize paying unnecessary exorbitant federal and state taxes, such as in the case of the beloved actor Gandolfini.

In my professional experience, the smoothest settling of estates was accomplished by parents that actually had a will reading in the presence of their children prior to their deaths.

Preparing Living Wills and Other Advance Notices

Before preparing a living will, the vocabulary of important words that usually confuse people should be studied and understood. The following are brief descriptions of words that are used in the preparation of a will and other important documents:

- **Living Wills**—these legal documents spell out the types of medical treatments and life-sustaining measures a person wants or doesn't want, such as mechanical breathing (respirator and ventilator), tube feeding, or resuscitation. A living will describes a person's preferences regarding treatments if faced with a serious accident or illness. **The document speaks for you when you are unable to speak for yourself.**

- **Medical or Health Care Power of Attorney (POA)**—The medical POA is a legal document that designates an individual, referred to as a health care agent or proxy, who will make medical decisions for a person if they are unable to do so. This POA should not be confused with a person who has the POA to make financial decisions. The medical POA will be guided by the living will but has the authority to interpret a person's wishes in situations that aren't covered in a living will. Choosing this person is possibly the most important part of the planning process; it should be a person that is trusted, has your interests at heart, understands your wishes, and will act in accordance with your advance written directives. The person should be mature and levelheaded, and comfortable dealing with death-related issues and conversations. **Never, never** pick someone out of feelings of guilt or obligation. Many people prefer not to have the same person as a financial and a medical POA.

- **Do not Resuscitate (DNR) Order**—this is invariably a very controversial topic within families. When the time comes to "pulling the plug," there are always family members that refuse to be instrumental in ending a loved one's life. Therefore, it's important to discuss with family members your wishes and let them understand your values, such as how important it is for you to be independent and self-sufficient, and what you feel would make your life not worth living. Let them know under what circumstances you want your life extended or terminated. Let them know if you want painkillers to ease your pain and discomfort if you are terminally ill. Explaining some of the terms that apply to DNR might be helpful at this point:

  - **Resuscitation**—this procedure restarts the heart when it has stopped beating by CPR or a device that delivers an electric shock to stimulate the heart. Many people are uncomfortable with having these procedures attempted, especially if they are very old, terminally ill, or have religious concerns.
  - **Mechanical Ventilation**—takes over breathing when a person is unable to do so. It's important that you stipulate how long you want to continue being on this life support.
  - **Nutritional and Hydration Assistance**—Supplies the body with nutrients and fluids intravenously or via a tube in the stomach. It should be made clear how long you might want to remain on this type of support.
  - **Dialysis**—Removes waste from your blood and manages fluid levels if your kidneys no longer function. Again, it should be made clear how long this procedure should be used.

Injury, illness, and death, at any age, aren't easy subjects to talk about openly, but planning ahead will ensure that your medical wishes will be followed, and will also relieve your family of the burden of trying to guess what your wishes were. Let them know that you have written advance directives and explain to them in detail what you want to happen when the time comes. It's also wise, to give the responsible parties a copy of all the death related documents soon after they are prepared.

When all of the essential documents are completed and your family is aware of your wishes, the only thing left for you to do is to make a detailed list of where all of your documents are and the names and telephone numbers of your contact people. A copy of this list should be given to all those responsible for carrying out your wishes, including your designated lawyers and accountants. I used an **Important Information Schedule** listing that I developed during my financial advisor days that included the following:

- My name, address, social security number, and date of birth.
- Where my safety deposit box is located and who has the keys and authority to access it.
- Where the original and copies of my wills and living wills are located.
- Names, addresses, and telephone numbers of my executors and trustees.
- Names, addresses, telephone numbers, and personal contacts at my brokerage accounts.
- Names, addresses, telephone numbers, and personal contacts at my checking and savings accounts.
- Name, address, and telephone number of the attorney that I wish to handle my estate.
- Name, address, and telephone number of the accountants that I wish to prepare documents and file tax returns that are required by law.
- Name, address, and telephone numbers of my doctors.
- Name, address, telephone number, and policy numbers of life insurance companies and my contacts, detailing the value of the insurance policies and the beneficiaries.
- Obituary information that I want used; this relieves a lot of tension for family members.

- Burial instruction and place of internment.

With all of the above accomplished, life after your death will become much easier for those remaining and will give them much more time to figure out how to successfully dispose of your assets amicably and in accordance with your wishes.

Getting Rid of Life's Treasures and Junk

I saved writing about one of the most distasteful chores of becoming a senior citizen for last, and that is getting rid of stuff. Our possessions are part of our history, and in some cases even part of our souls. We have baby shoes from our kids; some are even bronzed and enshrined in a sacred place in our home. We have baby clothes that we refused to relinquish as they all have a special place in our hearts and memories, and when we see and touch them, memories flash into our minds as we relive the soft feeling of their bodies and their baby powdered scent. We have souvenirs from our travels that keep reminding us of how sweet it was to be young and adventuresome. I could go on and on, but I think I've said enough on the subject, as I too get emotional when I think of all the precious memorable possessions that we had to get rid of.

Over our lifetimes, we accumulate an amazing amount of things that we treasure. It seems that we are pack rats by nature and find it very difficult to get rid of our bountiful accumulation. Everyone is different when it comes to getting rid of things, so I'll relate how we began getting rid of our possessions over the past few years, with some degree of success:

- **Old Tax Returns**—it took me months to go through all the tax returns that I filed since I was married in 1964. My files included cancelled checks, charitable receipts, proof of payments, diaries, and stock receipts. My filing cabinets were bulging with ancient history that I so foolishly accumulated in the event that I might somehow have to refer to information sometime in the future. I now only have the last seven years tax returns and have thrown out all of the unnecessary paperwork pertaining to those years. It took weeks to shred the old documents, reminiscing about those precious years as I placed each piece of my past into recycling bags.

- **Old Photos**—In addition to the multitude of photo albums that we have, we managed to accumulate hundreds of pictures of family and friends that ended up in several cardboard boxes in our basement. What to do with these precious gems? Well, Barbara and I spent several weeks sorting through them, reminiscing while placing them in separate piles for our two children, ten nephew and nieces and our other relatives and friends. We delivered the photos, neatly boxed and wrapped in Xmas paper to them, and presented the gifts at Christmas time. A big hit were the baby pictures of my nieces and nephews that they had never seen along with pictures of their parents when they were in their prime of life.

- **Old Videos**—What to do with the hundreds of Super 8 films and video tapes that accumulated over the years and were placed in a sacred place never to be viewed again? It took us months to review reels of film and tapes. Sorting them by the person we wished to receive our gems took longer than we anticipated, but was worth the effort. The only problem remaining was how to present our relatives with so many pieces of history? Barbara had a brainstorm; a young neighbor had the right equipment and volunteered to transfer the reels and tapes onto DVDs. We worked out financial arrangements and within a couple of months, he finished the job to perfection. After the enormous undertaking was over, we presented our relatives with the discs as Xmas presents. Their reaction was overwhelming and they rewarded us with lots of hugs and kisses and many phone calls of appreciation after they viewed precious family moments that were caught on film.

- **Clothing**—How do I begin to explain the number of suits, jackets, slacks, shirts, ties, dresses and shoes that we accumulated over the years? The big question was, which do we get rid of? It was a lot easier for me to dispose of my collection, as it seemed that most of my clothing didn't fit my ancient body. But Barbara still had her girlish figure and parting with her garments was a traumatic experience for her. Many a blouse and dress that went into the donation pile ended up back in her closet or in the new space that miraculously appeared in my emptied closets that she insisted had to be filled with her clothing. Most of my stuff went to the homeless shelter at the Salvation Army and was received with lots of gratitude. Barbara's small pile of stuff went to the Lupus Society to be sold at their various outlets to assist in their research programs.

- **Books, Books, Books, and more Books**—I couldn't believe the number of books that we collected over our 40 years of marriage. Barbara made a habit of recycling many of her books to her friends, but I never could part with a book once it was in my possession. As I wrote previously, most of my books were on the topic of "Christopher Columbus and the Age of Discovery." I was fortunate to place most, but not all, of my collections of over 400 books and documents at the Columbus Foundation in New York City where it currently resides in the Mike Bivona Library. Giving away my gems was one of my saddest experiences, but it was a better choice than having them disbursed to unknown places after my demise.

Although I was not able to convince my wife to give the girls in our family some of her jewelry, I was able to convince her to make a list of what she had and who would be the recipients of the heirlooms after her demise.

What's really surprising, is that after going through all the heartaches of disposing of our precious and not so precious possessions, we still have a house full of **stuff** that needs to be disposed of.

Oh well, tomorrow is another day...

C H A P T E R T W E L V E

Beneficial Organizations for Retirees

My wife and I subscribe to email information organizations that keep us abreast with topics we are interested in. Most are free and only require filling out online forms. My wife's favorite is *iVillage* at <u>www.iVillage.com</u>. It is a media company that is owned by NBC Universal Inc. The site focuses on categories targeted at women, including Entertainment, Beauty and Style, Family, Food, and Health. The site has approximately 34 million visitors a month (per comScore, April 2010). Barbara enjoys reading the weekly emails that cover topics that are not only of interest to her, but have also captured my attention as well. Part of a recent headline was:

"Don't Be a Morning Stiff! 15 Stretches to Start Your Day Off."

Let's face it, getting motivated in the morning isn't always easy. A cup of coffee and a few feel-good stretches can help. "Muscles stiffen overnight from lack of movement," says Leslie Wakefield D.P.T, doctor of physical therapy with Clear Passage Physical Therapy, Miami, FL "This results in stiffness of the connective tissue (known as fascia) as well as the muscles."

The article follows with three basic types of stretches:

For connective Tissue:

1-The three-in-one

Lie on your back with your arms outstretched, so that your body is in the shape of a T. Bend both knees and bring your right ankle on the left knee, creating a triangle shape between your legs. Keeping your shoulders in place, allow your legs to roll to the left while keeping that triangle intact, then repeat on the opposite side.

2-Hip flexor stretch

Scoot to the edge of your bed so that your side lines up with the side of your bed. Let your leg drop off the side and hug the other knee to your chest to support your lower back. You should feel a stretch through the front of your hanging leg's thigh and hip, then repeat on the other side.

3-Child's pose

Kneel in bed then sit back so that your bum is resting on your heels. Gently bend forward until your head touches the mattress. If you need to, fold your arms in front of your face to support your head. Otherwise, reach your arms forward to open connective tissue throughout the shoulders and back.

The rest of the exercise details can be found on their website. I'll just highlight the main areas so your can get an idea of how thorough and professional the information is:

- **For Muscles:**
  - o   **Triple neck stretch**
  - o   **Wall-push calf stretch**

- o **Chest stretch**
- o **Low-back stretch**
- o **Hip rotation stretch (lower back)**
- o **Seated hamstring**
- **For joints and circulation:**
  - o **Down-dog with Swan**
  - o **Inchworm**
  - o **Trunk twist**

It was easy for my wife to put some of the above suggestions to good use. I also have successfully incorporated some of the above stretches into my morning routine with pretty good results.

Another favorite of ours is *Let Life In—The 50+ Magazine* at www. letlifein.com. Gary Geyer, Chief Editor, describes the essence of his magazine as follows:

> There is a tendency today to lump all boomers together as if we're some sort of club. The boomer label implies that we are all the same and that our feelings and experiences are the same, which of course is not true. It shouldn't be a surprise that we who are over 50 are many things besides being over 50.
>
> *Let Life In* deals with the realities, not the myths, of being a boomer today. At *Let Life In*, you'll find we don't mince words or beat around the bush. Unlike other websites directed to the "after 50" audience, the writers and editors whose expertise comprise the content of this site don't sugar-coat the 50+ years but reveal what boomers today, as individuals, are thinking, exploring and experiencing.
>
> *Let Life In is* about the years after 50, without the B.S.

Some of the topics covered in the emagazine are:

- Relationships
- Sex After 50

- Retirement
- Grand Parenting
- Looking Back
- Health & Wellbeing
- Famous People 50+
- Vacations & Travel
- Fun Stuff
- Members' Stories

Some articles from members have been:

- Still a Hippie at Heart
- Should I Eat Before I Exercise in the Morning?
- Demise of the Donut Hole
- Betty and Veronica, A Rare Female Friendship
- A Mobility Scooter = Freedom and Independence
- Don't Call me Grandma
- Overcoming Anxieties of Dating Again after 50
- Grieving the Death of a Friend
- Warning, Retirement may be Stressful
- Falling in Love While Grieving
- How Women can Maintain Sexual Self Esteem after 50

As we can see from the above articles, there is an abundance of firsthand information by seniors over 50 who share their concerns and provide information that is commonly of interest to others in their age group.

Again, there is no subscription charge for joining the 50+ email group. We tried it and have become devoted fans.

Military Organizations

Military and veteran associations provide an abundance of services and opportunities for veterans, those on active-duty, in the reserves, and the National Guard. In addition to offering benefits to members of the military community, past and present, many offer services for family members as well. A directory of these military/veteran associations and organizations can be found at www.military.com. It lists the type and service affiliation under the broad categories of:

Army-Veterans & Military Retiree Associations

Navy-Spouse & Family Support Organizations

Air Force-Trade & Career Associations

Marine Corps-Veteran Service Organizations

Coast Guard-State Defense Forces and Civilian Militias

As a former member of the United States Air Force, I joined the Air Force Association (AFA) soon after concluding my four-year commitment. Their website is www.afa.org/about where I gleaned the following information:

> AFA is led by volunteer leaders at the national, state, and local levels. AFA's state organizations have more than 230 chapters that hold elections and conduct programs to increase the public's understanding of key national security issues in their communities. AFA publishes a monthly *Air Force Magazine,* conducts national symposia, and disseminates information through outreach programs. It sponsors professional development seminars and recognizes excellence in the education and aerospace fields through national awards programs. AFA presents scholarships and grants to Air Force active duty, Air National Guard, and Air Force Reserve members and their dependents; and awards educator grants to promote science and math education at the elementary and secondary school levels.

Some of the AFA membership benefits are:

- **Insurance**-including life, accident, auto, Tricare supplements, etc.
- **Financial**-including banking, financial planning and advice and credit card services.

- **Legal Services**-through the Hyatt Group.
- **Health**-dental, prescription discounts, hearing benefits, vision, and lifeline screening.
- **Shopping Discounts**-including Dell & Apple products. (In addition to getting discounts for computers that we purchased, we have used the AFA code to get discounts for our home and auto policies.)
- **Career**-resume' assistance.
- **Education**-SAT/ACT discounts through www. eKnowledge.com/AFA
- **Travel**-Exclusive Worldwide Hotel Discount Programs, Government Vacation Rewards, truck and car rental discounts, and numerous other discounts, can be found at www.afa.com.

Over the years Barbara and I have saved thousands of dollars using the AFA code. The other military organizations have similar types of benefits that should be explored for the many money saving opportunities and the guidance that it affords its members.

For those who require up-to-date financial information and a good stocks and bonds tracking system, Morningstar at www.morningstar. com offers some free subscriptions for basic information, and an annual membership fee for more in-depth data. We have used their services for over 20 years to our advantage and will continue to do so into the foreseeable future. Wikipedia describes their operations nicely:

> Morningstar provides data on approximately 456,000 investment offerings, including stocks, mutual funds, and similar vehicles, along with real-time global market data on more than 12 million equities, indexes, futures, options, commodities, and precious metals, in addition to foreign exchange and Treasury markets. Morningstar also offers investment management services through its registered investment advisor subsidiaries and has approximately $164 billion in

assets under advisement and management, as of March 31, 2014. The company has operations in 27 countries.

Morningstar created the Morningstar Rating, Morningstar Analyst Rating, Morningstar Style Box, and other proprietary financial measurements.

With approximately $164 billion in assets under management and advisement, it provides comprehensive **retirement,** investment advisory, portfolio management, and index services for financial institutions, plan sponsors, and advisors around the world.

It's very comforting to have such a sophisticated organization available when researching prospective security purchases. The information that they offer is detailed beyond what many other companies offer. An extremely useful feature is their monitoring advisory alert system that informs subscribers about timely news on securities that are on an investors tracking list.

Before concluding this section, I would like to remind readers that AARP, as discussed in Chapter Nine, should be one of the first organizations that seniors join, as its benefits far outweigh their small annual membership fee. Even the First Lady of the United States, Michelle Obama, became a member on her 50th birthday in 2014. AARP proudly features a picture of her holding her membership card on their website. So, regardless of your political affiliation, what's good for the First Lady. . . .

CHAPTER THIRTEEN

What Have We Learned?

It is easy to look back and determine what we should have done differently to make our retirement and life an easier and more productive journey. Hindsight is wonderful; it allows us to put ourselves at perfect places in a perfect world. But life is not perfect and we have all made decisions that, if given a chance, we would have made differently. I can't speak for others, but I can draw from our experiences about the things we should have done to make our lives and those of our loved ones more comfortable.

The three most important segments of our existence that affected our retirement were **health**, **attitude**, and **finances**. Barbara and I, after long discussions and debates, agreed that if we could relive our younger days, we certainly would have done many things differently.

We know that, at this time in our lives, the most important thing is staying healthy so we can get the most out of life and be there for the people who mean so much to us. We asked ourselves what we should have done differently to have accomplished this. There is no doubt that we should have been more proactive when it came to:

1) **Having annual medical check-ups.** I'm sure that we all did the same thing in our younger days when we felt invincible. The only time we visited a doctor's office was when we didn't feel well. Barbara and I began having annual check-ups

after we both had life-threatening illnesses. I'm sure that if I had made earlier visits to doctors that my open heart surgery at age 59 may have been avoided or postponed to a time when alternative methods, such as artery stents or improved medications, were developed that could have been a lot less intrusive and dangerous. I don't know if Barbara's brain aneurysm operation could have been avoided, but the problem may have been detected sooner and handled accordingly, maybe under less critical and life threatening circumstances. Now that we are wiser, we practice preventive medical care. We have flu and pneumonia shots regularly and take cholesterol and other tests that may detect abnormalities frequently, before they become serious and possibly life-threatening. At this writing, I'm a victim of shingles. Over the years, when asked if I wanted that shot, my answer was always the same, "I never had the chicken pox, so I don't need the shot." Well, I'm now in my fourth month since the rash and blisters appeared on my chest and back. In two weeks they were gone, but the pain is still with me even though I've tried all kinds of recommended medications and treatments. My advice is whether or not you've had the chicken pox, that it's a good idea to have the shingles vaccine, with your doctor's permission, of course.

2) **Developing the right attitude.** As our tango mentor impressed on us when we visited Buenos Aires to learn the Argentine Tango: "The right attitude in dancing and life is the essence of our existence." When we were young, we let many unimportant things dictate our actions and the level of stress we put ourselves under. The pressure of our jobs always played a central role in how we behaved while working and in our homes. It would have been nice if we'd learned to let important and unimportant things that created stress in our lives roll off our shoulders and had dealt with them as if they were natural and normal events in our lives. Looking back, it seems as if the little unhappy events created as much stress as the major ones, both having the same effect on us. I think

if we would have taken dance lessons and had been in exercise programs when we were younger, that we would have worked off lots of unwelcomed stress on the dance floor and gym, and would have developed a healthier attitude towards life with a lot less stress.

3) **Financial Considerations.** Barbara and I were born during the Great Depression (1929-1939). Although we were both too young to remember that period, we were brought up in families that carried with them memories of those hard times and they passed their concerns on to us. So, what does that have to do with financial matters during retirement? Well, the lesson I learned from the many financial recessions and near depressions that I've witnessed is that I should have paid more attention to what people who experienced the Great Depression said. Some of the advice that my parents drilled into me was: "A fool and his gold are soon parted," "A penny saved is a penny earned," "There is no such thing as becoming rich overnight," "Remember that someone trying to sell you something is doing so for his benefit, not yours," and, "If it seems too good to be true then it's probably not true." The cautious advice I received in my youth goes on and on. What it took me to learn when I was in my 50s would have saved me lots of money and grief if I applied the same strategy when I was in my 30s. As mentioned previously, investing your age, let's say 30% in safe interest bearing bonds at age 30, and 40% at age 40, and the remainder, 70% and 60% respectively, in high quality dividend paying stocks, would have avoided many sleepless nights and would have done wonders for my retirement funds. Many times when I tried to make a "killing" in the stock market or a "quick buck" in business, I ended being killed and losing money, which was always followed by unwelcomed stress for me and my family.

I hope, in some way, that my writing, based on our experiences, will help current and future retirees smooth their paths into a more stable and secure retirement, as free as possible from unnecessary stress and hopefully with more than enough money to make their journey into the next phase of their lives one that they hoped for.

An important thing to remember is that if a person retires at age 60, and assuming he began work at age 20, it means that the 40 years spent in the workforce may almost be matched by a similar number of years in retirement. So having financial stability and a plan of what to do in that final stage of life should begin well in advance of retirement.

Printed in the United States
By Bookmasters